BA

Thirty-Three Ways to Help with Numeracy

Thirty-Three Ways to Help with . . .

Series Editor: Linda Evans

This series of practical 'how-to' books is for teachers, teaching assistants and SENCOs who are in need of fresh ideas to teach pupils in their care who are struggling with basic skills. Each title provides tools enabling practitioners to make good provision for a range of children in their class. Practical ideas and materials can be extracted without needing to plough through chapters of theory and research.

All titles are A4 in format, photocopiable, and include an introduction and clearly presented activity pages.

Written by experienced practitioners and experts, this series is a lifeline to anyone facing the challenge of teaching children who are struggling.

Titles in the series so far:

Thirty-Three Ways to Help with Numeracy by Brian Sharp
Thirty-Three Ways to Help with Reading by Raewyn Hickey

Thirty-Three Ways to Help with Numeracy

Brian Sharp

Routledge
Taylor & Francis Group

LONDON AND NEW YORK

First published 2009
by Routledge
2 Park Square, Milton Park, Abingdon, Oxon, OX14 4RN

Simultaneously published in the USA and Canada
by Routledge
270 Madison Avenue, New York, NY 10016

Routledge is an imprint of the Taylor & Francis Group, an informa business

© 2009 Brian Sharp

Typeset in Bembo by Keystroke,
28 High Street, Tettenhall, Wolverhampton
Printed and bound in Great Britain by
Antony Rowe Ltd, Chippenham, Wiltshire

British Library Cataloguing in Publication Data
A catalogue record for this book is available from the British Library

Library of Congress Cataloging-in-Publication Data
Sharp, Brian.
    Thirty three ways to help with numeracy / Brian Sharp.
        p. cm.
    1. Numeracy—Study and teaching (Elementary)—Activity programs.
2. Counting—Study and teaching (Elementary)—Activity programs.
3. Arithmetic—Remedial teaching. I. Title. II. Title: 33 ways to help
with numeracy.
    QA141.15.S53 2008
    372.7—dc22   2008014896

ISBN 10: 0–415–46896–5
ISBN 13: 978–0–415–46896–1

Contents

The series   vii

Acknowledgements   ix

Introduction   xi

A. Beginning with counting   1
Activities:

  1. Reach the moon   3

  2. Arrays of counters   6

  3. Magic three, four, five   9

  4. Counting across a square   13

  5. Journeys on a hundred square   16

  6. Pyramids 1   21

  7. Pyramids 2   24

B. Developing counting and finding the value of numbers   28
Activities:

  8. Ten is greater than one   29

  9. From counting to number lines   32

10. Sequences of counters   35

11. The value of money   38

12. Counting small amounts of money   41

13. Place value grids   44

C. Developing images to support calculation   48
Activities:

14. Complements to ten   50

15. Using number lines for addition   53

16. Introducing number lines for subtraction: numbers up to ten | 56
17. Using number lines for subtraction: numbers over twenty | 59
18. Using number lines for subtraction: difference is greater than ten | 62
19. Giving change | 65
20. Make a rectangle | 68
21. Factor walls | 76
22. Using number lines for multiplication | 79
23. Using number lines for division | 82
24. Multiplying with cards and counters | 85

D. Organising thinking to aid calculation | **90**
Activities:

25. Reordering to find complements | 91
26. Partitioning | 93
27. Piecing together multiplication tables | 97

E. Time | **100**
Activities:

28. Wheels of time | 101
29. Fractions of time | 106

F. Understanding fractions | **109**
Activities:

30. Cuisenaire fractions: numbers up to ten | 111
31. Bars of chocolate | 115
32. Fractions of a number line | 118
33. Images of fractions, using parts of a circle | 122

Thirty-three ways to help . . . the series

This is a series of books to help teachers, teaching assistants and parents who want to help children to learn.

Most children at some stage or other in their school life come across something that they find difficult; a small minority of learners have difficulty in grasping the basic ideas presented in many lessons. Whatever the case, there is a need then for extra explanation and practice so that children can unravel any misconceptions, understand what is being taught and move on. Very often nowadays, this extra practice – or 'reinforcement' – is provided by teaching assistants (TAs) who are such a valuable resource in our schools.

Planning activities for TAs to use with children who need extra help can be challenging, however. There is little time for teachers to design 'mini-lessons' for TAs to use with individuals or small groups of children – and to talk them through the 'delivery' of such activities. This is exactly where the **thirty-three ways** series comes into play.

Teachers will be able to choose an appropriate activity for individuals or groups as part of their structured programme, or as a 'one-off' lesson for extra practice. The games and activities require no prior theoretical reading or knowledge and only a little preparation, so can be easily used by TAs or volunteer helpers in the classroom; teachers may also wish to share some activities with parents who want to know how to support their children at home. The activities use a multi-sensory approach to learning – visual, auditory and kinaesthetic; they have been designed for children aged 6–11years, who need additional help with particular skills and concepts.

Teachers are constantly challenged to find ways to keep pupils motivated and to give them worthwhile 'catch-up' opportunities. But much of the photocopiable material available to teachers is too often 'busy work' which keeps children 'occupied' as opposed to learning. The books in this series provide a variety of adult-led activities that will keep children interested and take them forward in their learning. In this way, their confidence and self esteem will grow as they experience success and have fun at the same time.

Series features

- Activities are practical (do not involve pencil-and-paper worksheets) and multi-sensory, to keep children motivated and enjoying learning.

- Activities do not require a lot of preparation and any materials required are readily available in classrooms.

- Activities are adult-led, so children do not have the opportunity to keep repeating the same mistakes.

- Activities are grouped into different basic skill areas, so teachers can choose the activity best suited for a child's needs.

- Clear, concise reasons are set out for each activity.

- An extension activity is given, where appropriate, to challenge pupils and extend their learning.

Acknowledgements

A resource such as this is directly and indirectly affected by both influence and support: influence from a variety of sources and support from a good many people in a good many different ways. I have been privileged to work among many inspiring colleagues in the mathematics education community – teachers in Hampshire, Shropshire and Herefordshire, and mathematics consultant colleagues from all over England as we support the National Strategy – and I thank them all. In particular I would like to thank influential figures such as Don Steward (mathematics adviser in Shropshire during my time there), Professor John Mason (Open University), Dr Anne Watson (University of Oxford), Malcolm Swan (University of Nottingham) and other writers such as David Wells and Geoff Giles, whose ways of developing powerful questioning have helped me to form my own views on how children should learn and can express their understanding. I would especially like to thank Professor Ian Thompson from Northumbria University, whose research on the use of the number lines (particularly with subtraction, seen in the DfES (2004) resource 'Progression from mental to calculator skills'[1]) caused me to think very clearly about how children's understanding can progress with calculations. This particular work on number lines was also developed by my Primary National Numeracy colleagues in Herefordshire, who at the time were Jane Churchill, Veronica Ruth and Linda Townsend, and to whom I also express my grateful thanks.

And, of course, I wish to say thank you to my family, Sue, Jamie, Daniel and Connor, who still show their love despite the times I create my own pressures when I take on projects because of ambition, when they know I should learn to relax sometimes and be happy.

Note

1 DfES (2004) Key Stage 3 National Strategy *Progression from mental to calculator skills*, DfES 0046–2004, London: DfES.

Introduction

Lots of us have difficulties with understanding mathematics – often because we are uncertain about our own thinking and reasoning skills, and our confidence is low. We might memorise various methods and 'tricks' of calculating, but don't really understand what the four operations – addition, subtraction, multiplication and division – actually mean. One example of this is when children see that $2 \times 10 = 20$, and $3 \times 10 = 30$, and they are told or they see for themselves that you always add a nought when multiplying by ten. Unfortunately, this leaves many children applying this rule with all numbers, including decimals, so that they believe that $2.5 \times 10 = 2.50$ because their *misconception* is not corrected or discussed. Such incomplete understanding often leads to a child becoming more and more confused and losing any confidence that the child may have had as far as numeracy goes.

The activities in this collection are designed to build learners' confidence by developing reasoning and thinking about physical number situations. Understanding develops through discussion, sharing views about what we have seen, thought and done, and through it learners can recognise that their own thinking is valid and worthwhile. It is in this way that we build the self-esteem of learners – a fundamental aspect of learning that must be at the heart of what we do.

The activities explore number by 'doing' – using a range of physical and visual resources, some of which relate number to other applications, such as lengths, money, area, circles and time. It is important that all learners enjoy an experience of the full range of mathematics, even when focusing on numeracy. In this way, links can be made between one aspect that can enhance understanding of another; for example, subtraction can be understood through complementary addition; an understanding of the five times table can help learners read time on analogue clocks; an understanding of area links with handling factors or multiples of numbers. Using these links enables learners to build their own mathematical structures to support their thinking when solving any problems they meet.

For this reason, it is best to use a range of activities when exploring calculations. For example, there are three linked multiplication activities – '20: Make a rectangle', '22: Using number lines for multiplication' and '24: Multiplying with cards and counters' – all giving different ways of looking at multiplication, but all useful in developing understanding. If exploring division, there appears to be only one activity: '23: Using number lines for division', but division links directly with multiplication, and so these activities would also support a better understanding of it.

The resources are explained in detail to enable you to prepare the sessions, and the activities suggest questions to ask, to help you check the learner's understanding and progress. *Questions* are written in *italics*, and **possible responses** are given in **bold type**. Of course, the most powerful question to ask is '*How did you work that out?*' for two reasons: it enables children to explain, so giving them the opportunity to understand their own methods and reasoning, and it enables you to see their thinking, so you can identify any misconceptions they may have. There are often extension or consolidation ideas listed that will help take the learning further. It is essential that teachers and TAs listen to children's responses to questions and observe their actions in learning situations in order to ascertain their understanding and progress, and possibly adapt an activity depending on the needs of the child. In this way, the teaching is responsive and more likely to be successful.

I hope that if you are working with a child who says '*I can't do maths*' then you can help them realise that they **can do** these activities and encourage them to begin to believe in their own abilities. I hope too, that using some or all of the activities in this collection is an enjoyable experience for both learners and teachers/teaching assistants.

A. Beginning with counting

Counting comes before an appreciation of the meaning of numerals. Within counting there is the assumed understanding that the objects we are counting are matched one to one with the numerals we say. Some children with difficulties in understanding number may say the numbers 1–2–3–4 etc., but not at the same time as touching the objects they are supposed to be counting. However, one-to-one matching is an essential stage of understanding the meaning of number, and without it the numerals carry little value.

The following activities give varied opportunities for counting 'with a purpose' and should be additional to any counting experiences you offer to children within the main class activities. Some activities provide the chance to count indoors at a desk or table, using counters, matchsticks or pens, or outside, where children can pace out a given number of steps, or use a metre rule.

Learners should be given a variety of opportunities to count, whether it is objects, or movement – such as the number of turns of the wheels of a wheelchair, or the number of spaces moved on a snakes and ladders board – or measurements, such as lengths in centimetres on a ruler or minutes on a clock. Games are particularly valuable experiences, because the counting is set in a fun context.

The following activities are found in this section:

1. **Reach the moon** – counting steps in different directions on a grid of square.

2. **Arrays of counters** – arranging counters in rectangles to highlight even and odd numbers, or showing special numbers such as tens or fives.

3. **Magic three, four, five** – counting along the lengths of the three sides of a triangle.

4. **Counting across a square** – counting along the sides and diagonal of a square.

5. **Journeys on a hundred square** – moving from one number to another, using a 100 square.

6. **Pyramids 1** – This activity links with Pyramids 2 and introduces addition and subtraction through counting.

7. **Pyramids 2**.

Reach the moon

This is an activity that combines counting with giving directions. It can be extended to using a maze.

This activity will help children to:

● use the words of movement – up, down, left, right

● count the number of squares as they move

● give or follow a sequence of instructions.

You will need these resources:

● some counters – one may be enough, but some children may wish to use a counter for each square of movement that they count

● the diagram shown on page 5, or a similar one of your own, using a square grid.

The activity

● Place the counter on the smiley face square of the diagram, and ask questions such as the following. The child can be encouraged to move the counter to reach the other objects.

What directions would you give to the smiley face to reach the moon?
Left 4, down 1.

What directions would you give to the smiley face to reach the cross?
Up 5, left 3.

What directions would you give to the smiley face to reach the heart?
Up 4, right 3.

- Add a drawing of your own in any one of the squares, and see if you can work out the directions you would give the smiley face to reach it.

Extension

- You could modify the diagram by shading in parts of it, like a maze below, placing the characters wherever you like.

Arrays of counters

This is a counting activity that can lead to an understanding of a range of mathematical ideas – including counting in twos, fives and/or tens, and recognising multiples. Eventually, this idea of arranging counters links to areas of rectangles. It will link with other activities – for example, '9. From counting to number lines' and '20. Make a rectangle'.

This activity will help children to:

- match counting with pointing to the object

- recognise even and odd numbers

- count objects – up to 10, 20 or whatever is appropriate

- recognise numbers in the two, five or ten times table.

You will need these resources:

- up to 50 counters in two colours

- paper and pencil to write next to the counters.

The activity

- Place the counters on the paper, arranging some of them in pairs, and ask the child to count with you. They should point to the counters as they count, for example:

1 ○ ● 2

3 ○ ● 4

5 ○ ● 6

What will the next number be? **7**.

What colour do you think the next counter will be?

What will the number after that be? **8**. *And its colour?*

- Recite the numbers of the dark coloured counters together: 2, 4, 6, 8. Can you carry on the sequence? **10**.

  Is there anything special about the numbers of the dark counters? **Even numbers**.

- Repeat for the odd numbers.

Extension

The task can be extended for other multiples – for example, the ten times table. This time set out the counters as below, counting them as you build. The tenth counter each time is a different colour.

- This time highlight each tenth one by writing down its number as you count with the child:

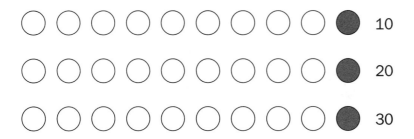

○ ○ ○ ○ ○ ○ ○ ○ ○ ● 10

○ ○ ○ ○ ○ ○ ○ ○ ○ ● 20

○ ○ ○ ○ ○ ○ ○ ○ ○ ● 30

What can you say about the numbers of the dark counters? **End in zero/all tens/ten times table.**

What would be the number of the next dark counter? **40.**

Can you carry on the sequence? **50, 60 etc.**

- After the twos and tens, children find the five times table the next step.

Magic three, four, five

This is a counting activity that produces a 'magic' result (attributed to Pythagoras), based on making three sides of a right-angled triangle.

The activity should help children to:

● match objects or steps with numbers

● count to 3, 4 and 5 (and beyond with extension activities).

You will need these resources:

● 12 matchsticks, pens or pencils

● an object that has a right angle, for example, a small square card

● paper and a ruler to draw straight lines as guidelines.

The activity could be conducted outside, in which case you will need a metre stick or you could step out paces. A large object (such as a cardboard box) can be used to make a right angle. The example below shows matchsticks, and uses a square shape for the right angle.

The activity

- Ask the child to count out three matches and lay them in a straight line:

- Then place a right-angled object to form the corner of the triangle:

- Then count out four more matches, and place them against the square, to form another side of the triangle:

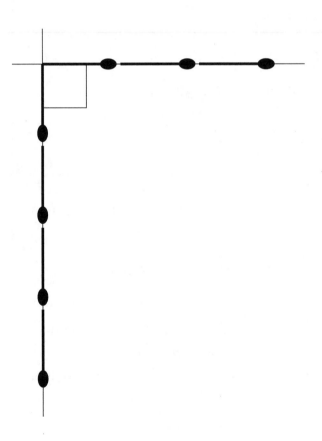

- Make a straight line between the two ends – either by drawing a line or placing a ruler between them – for example:

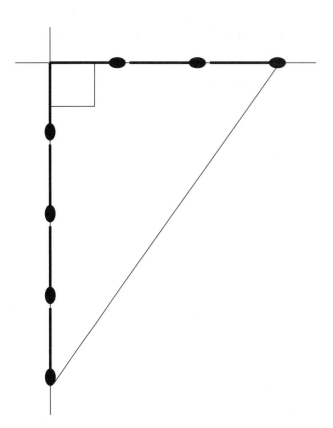

- We have five matches left. *Do they fit exactly along the line?* **Yes!**

- Try it out!

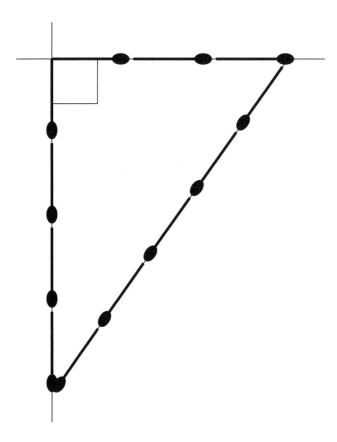

- Try the activity with different objects that are all the same length – pens, pencils, spoons, or outside with a metre stick. As long as the right angle is between the sides of lengths 3 and 4, then 5 will make the final side of the triangle. There are other numbers that will work in the same way – for example, 6, 8 and 10, or 5, 12 and 13, if the child is ready to count that far.

Counting across a square

This is another counting activity, this time involving building a square and counting the lengths of the sides. It also introduces the idea that the diagonal is longer than the sides (a common misconception among many children is that the diagonal of a square is the same length as the side).

The activity should help children to:

● match objects or steps with numbers

● count out numbers of objects up to ten

● begin to work with lengths that are not whole numbers.

You will need these resources:

● up to 60 matchsticks, pens or pencils

● an object that has a right angle, for example, a small square card

● possibly a large piece of paper and a ruler to draw straight lines as guidelines as you go along.

The activity could be conducted outside, in which case you will need a metre stick or you could step out paces. A large object (such as a cardboard box) can be used to make a right angle. The example below shows matchsticks, and uses a square shape for the right angle.

The activity

- Ask the child to count out five matches and lay them out in a straight line:

- Then place a right-angled object to form the corner of the triangle that is going to be made – here a square card is used:

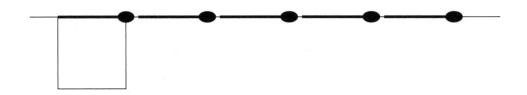

- Then count out five more matches, and form another side of the square:

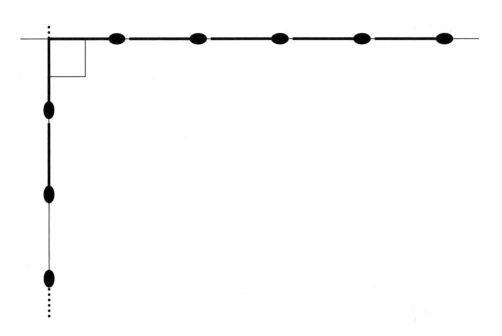

- Then, build the whole square with five matches on each side.

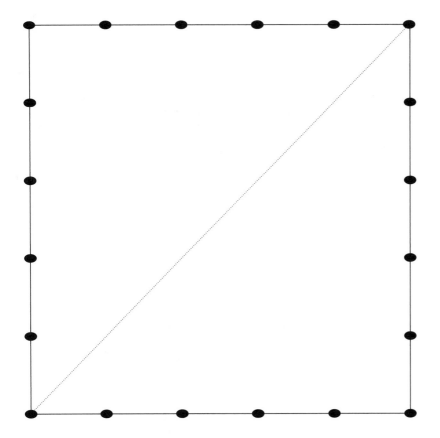

How long is each side? **5**.

Are all the sides the same length? **Yes**.

How many matches will we use to go across the square in a diagonal (along the dotted line on the diagram)? Try it out! **(The answer is about 7.)**

If you try the activity with different objects (all with a consistent length), the result will be the same, but it is a good opportunity for children to count different objects up to 5 each time. It is especially good to try the activity outside, pacing out the square, but making sure that the paces are the same length as far as is possible.

- Try with other size squares. However, note that no square built in this way will give an exact whole number answer for the diagonal:

- A square with side 3 will have a diagonal of about 4.

- A square with side 7 will have a diagonal of about 10.

- A square with side 10 will have a diagonal of about 14.

Journeys on a hundred square

The hundred square offers another visual structure, and we can use it here to help find the difference between two numbers. Note that the numbers can be organised from top to bottom, or, as here, from bottom to top.

This activity will help children to:

- count on in ones from one number to another

- count on in tens from one number to another

- count forwards *and* backwards

- notice that the difference between, for example, 2 and 8 is the same as 12 and 18, and begin to reason why this is so.

You will need these resources:

- at most, five counters, each in a different colour

- a hundred square. Many are commercially available, but one is provided here that can be photocopied and laminated. You may wish to enlarge it to A3.

The activity

- Place one counter on the hundred square at a low number, and another at a slightly higher number. You may wish to start in the numbers 1–10 as follows:

91	92	93	94	95	96	97	98	99	100
81	82	83	84	85	86	87	88	89	90
71	72	73	74	75	76	77	78	79	80
61	62	63	64	65	66	67	68	69	70
51	52	53	54	55	56	57	58	59	60
41	42	43	44	45	46	47	48	49	50
31	32	33	34	35	36	37	38	39	40
21	22	23	24	25	26	27	28	29	30
11	12	13	14	15	16	17	18	19	20
1	2	3	4	5	6	7	8	9	10

- Move your counter from the 2 to the 8, counting each square. *How many places do you have to count to move from the 2 to the 8?* **6**. You may repeat this with any other pair of numbers in the first decade.

- An alternative question to help counting would be:

  If I start at 3, and count on six places, where do I end up? **9**.

The activity progresses by using numbers in the same decade – later we will try to highlight patterns by repeating the same units in other decades.

- For example, place one counter at 12 and the other at 18. *How many places do we count to move from 12 to 18?* **6 again**.

Why is it the same as when the counters were at 2 and 8?

- To help the child talk about this, you may wish to place counters at each of 2, 8 12 and 18, to show that the difference is the same between 2 to 8 and 12 to 18:

91	92	93	94	95	96	97	98	99	100
81	82	83	84	85	86	87	88	89	90
71	72	73	74	75	76	77	78	79	80
61	62	63	64	65	66	67	68	69	70
51	52	53	54	55	56	57	58	59	60
41	42	43	44	45	46	47	48	49	50
31	32	33	34	35	36	37	38	39	40
21	22	23	24	25	26	27	28	29	30
11	⬤	13	14	15	16	17	⬤	19	20
1	⬤	3	4	5	6	7	⬤	9	10

→

6

- Repeat this further up the hundred square – for example, for 22 to 28, 62 to 68 etc.

What is the difference between these numbers each time? **6**.

Extensions

- The next stage is to count in tens. Place the counters at, say, 4 and 14.

How many places do we move from 4 to 14? **10**.

- Children often count all ten singly. Repeat the question for 5 to 15, or 7 to 17, and point out that these differences are always ten. Place the counter at another number and ask the child to place their counter at the number that is ten more.

    Where is the number that is ten more than 4? **Just above it at 14**.

    Where is the number that is ten more than 5? **Just above it at 15**.

    What do you notice about all the numbers that are ten more? **Always one place above**.

    Compare the two numbers 4 and 14 – what is the same? **The four (in the units column)**.

    What is different? **14 has a ten in it. The one stands for ten**.

- Develop the activity towards counting in tens, for example, 4 and 24, 6 and 36, etc.

    What is the difference between 4 and 24? **20**.

    How many places above do we go? **Two places**. *How many tens is that?* **Two**.

Counting backwards

- If children count forwards confidently, then an important next step is to count backwards, at first in ones, then in tens. Repeat the activities above, this time counting down from the higher number to the lower.

100	99	98	97	96	95	94	93	92	91
90	89	88	87	86	85	84	83	82	81
80	79	78	77	76	75	74	73	72	71
70	69	68	67	66	65	64	63	62	61
60	59	58	57	56	55	54	53	52	51
50	49	48	47	46	45	44	43	42	41
40	39	38	37	36	35	34	33	32	31
30	29	28	27	26	25	24	23	22	21
20	19	18	17	16	15	14	13	12	11
10	9	8	7	6	5	4	3	2	1

Pyramids 1

This activity makes links between numbers – helping children to see addition links as well as differences between numbers.

This activity will help children to:

- count numbers of counters, and then add these numbers together

- link addition and subtraction, encouraging them to practise mental skills.

You will need these resources:

- up to 100 counters

- up to six containers for them, such as cups, saucers or jam-pot lids.

The activity

- Set out the counters as below, and ask the child to count how many there are in each container.

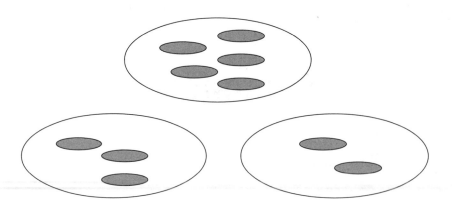

What links the numbers of counters in the lower two containers with the number of counters in the top one? **There are five counters alto-gether in the bottom containers, and five in the top one.**

● Try with other numbers of counters, making sure that the link stays the same; for example, place seven counters in the top one, and four and three counters in the bottom two.

Is there still the same number of counters in the top as the bottom two? **Yes**.

● Now place counters to show in only the bottom two containers, for example:

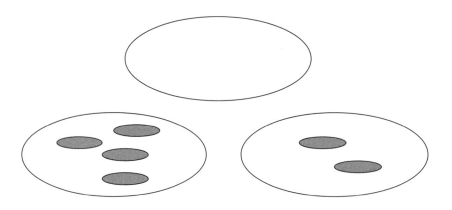

How many counters should be in the top one? **Six**.

How do you work it out? **Adding together the 4 and the 2**.

● Repeat with other numbers of counters.

Extension 1: linking addition and subtraction

- Develop the activity by leaving the counters out of one of the bottom containers, for example:

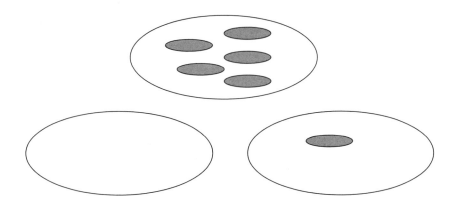

How many counters should there be in the empty container? **Four**.

Children may need guidance here: it may be that we have to get them to place counters in the empty container, and ask if they have the right number. Start with one counter, asking if there are enough, then two, and so on.

Extension 2

- You can extend the number of containers you use to either give more practice of adding, or, by leaving gaps, practice of subtratction.

    How many counters should be in the empty containers? **Three in the bottom one, and eight in the top one**.

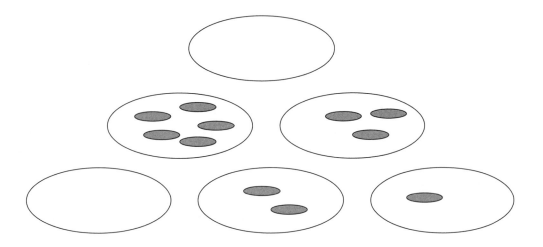

Pyramids 2

This activity builds on the ideas of Pyramids 1, but assumes that children are familiar with numbers rather than have a need to count physical objects. It is a popular activity often used in schools.

It will help children to:

- link addition and subtraction, encouraging them to practise mental skills.

You will need these resources:

- a set of cards with numbers written on them. You can choose to just use numbers up to ten, or go further up to 20 if appropriate. The hexagon numbers on p. 27 are provided to help, as they fit together nicely.

The activity

- Have a set of cards ready to use which are spread out so that pupils can see the ones they wish to choose. Set out some of the cards in the following arrangement and discuss how the numbers are connected.

    For example, here is $3 + 1 = 4$, but also we could say that $4 - 3 = 1$ or $4 - 1 = 3$.

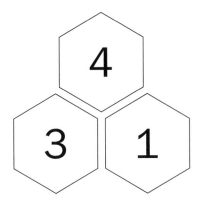

Can you find another set of three cards that link in the same way?

Can you make lots of different sets of three cards that work in the same way?

Here is a larger pyramid. Can you make a pyramid with other numbers that works like this?

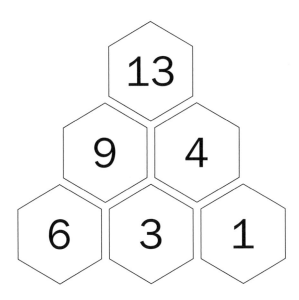

● You can turn the cards over, to hide some of the numbers. For example: *What number is hidden here?* **10**.

  How can you work it out? **7 + 3 = 10**.

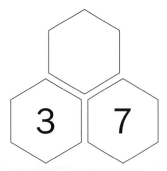

- Change this activity by turning over one of the bottom cards, to bring in subtraction. For example:

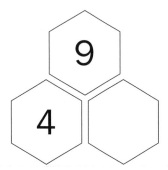

- Extend this activity with different sets of three (or six) cards. This can become quite challenging in larger pyramids if many gaps are left.

Pyramid investigation

What number would you get on the top of this pyramid?

If you change the order of the bottom three numbers, do you still get the same number at the top? (For example, 3 then 1 then 2 along the bottom.)

What is the largest number you can get at the top, if you have the 1,2 and 3 cards at the bottom, but in any order you choose?

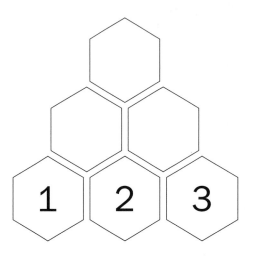

Hexagon numbers

1   2   3   4   5

6   7   8   9   10

11   12   13   14   15

16   17   18   19   20

21   22   23   24   25

26   27   28   29   30

B. Developing counting and finding the value of numbers

We never leave counting, but children need to apply this early skill in new ways – for example, by learning to count in twos, fives and tens, consolidating their understanding by ordering numbers, learning how to count money and beginning to understand place value.

The activities here also begin to connect counting with using number lines, and the hundred square as two examples of visual ways of supporting their understanding.

The following activities are found in this section:

8. **Ten is greater than one** – comparing lengths to link with the value of numbers.

9. **From counting to number lines** – introducing the number line for the first time.

10. **Sequences of counters** – organising counters in twos, threes etc. to aid counting in these numbers.

11. **The value of money** – illustrating the value of coins by using positions on a number line.

12. **Counting small amounts of money** – counting in coin values – ones, twos, fives, tens, etc. – and also organising the coins to aid counting.

13. **Place value grids** – understanding the value of the tens and the units in numbers, using parts of the hundred square.

Ten is greater than one

This is perhaps one of the simplest but most effective activities for learning about the value of numbers. Numbers are used in length as well as quantity, and this activity helps children compare lengths to get a feel for the relative sizes of numbers.

This activity will help children to:

● order numbers

● compare pairs of lengths.

You will need these resources:

● Cuisenaire rods are best for this activity, but the resource sheet of the lengths from 1 cm to 10 cm on page 31 could be used. Copy the sheet onto card and carefully cut out one of each length. You may wish to colour the cards for easier recognition; if so, the standard Cuisenaire colours are: 1 cm – white, 2 cm – red, 3 cm – light green, 4 cm – pink or purple, 5 cm – yellow, 6 cm – dark green, 7 cm – black, 8 cm – brown (or tan), 9 cm – blue, 10 cm – orange.

● if using rods, number ten small sticky labels with the numbers 1 to 10 on them, placing them appropriately onto the correct rods. The appropriate numbers are already printed on the resource sheet.

The activity

● Ask the child to place the lengths in order of size, for example:

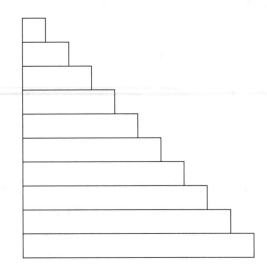

Which is the greatest? **10 cm**.

Point to the smallest length – what length is it? **1 cm**.

Can you say the order of the numbers? **1, 2, 3, 4, 5, 6, 7, 8, 9, 10**.
(Point to the numbers on the lengths as the child says these.)

● Now take a pair of lengths – for example, the 7 cm and 8 cm.

Can you put these together to find which is the longer? **8 cm**.

● Try with other pairs of your choice.

If you wish to use colour, the standard scheme for these rods is as follows:
1 cm – white, 2 cm – red, 3 cm – light green, 4 cm – pink or purple, 5 cm – yellow,
6 cm – dark green, 7 cm – black, 8 cm – brown (or tan), 9 cm – blue, 10 cm – orange.

From counting to number lines

One of the difficulties that children experience with number is that they are presented with different representations of numbers without having these representations linked. This activity transfers the counting of counters to number lines, building children's skills in counting in ones to 10, or counting in twos, fives and tens up to 20 or 100.

This activity will help children to:

- match counting objects to numbers on a number line

- prepare children for using the number line for calculations in later activities.

The extension looks at counting in twos and fives.

You will need these resources:

- up to 20 counters – 10 of each of two colours

- a number line where the scale is matched to the diameters of the counters, for example:

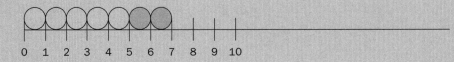

Depending on the support the child needs, not all the numbers need to be marked in, for example:

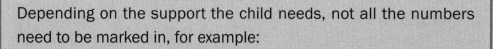

The activity

- Begin by ensuring that the child can match the words of counting with touching or moving the counters. Start with five counters.

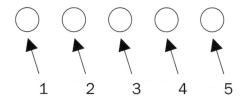

- This 1–1 matching is fundamental to counting and has to be understood first. Sometimes, children will be able to match up to three objects with the words, but later numbers become mere chants not matched with objects – build the skill of matching up to five counters initially, then on to ten. Next, move the counters together in a line, and count again.

- Then, move the counters onto the number line, one at a time, and ask the child to count, pointing to the numbers on the line as you go along.

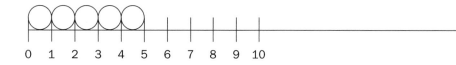

Extension, progression and alternative perspectives

- This technique may be used to help children count in twos, fives or tens. for example, by using two different colours, the twos can be highlighted:

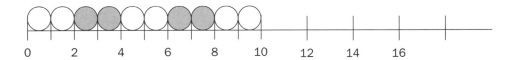

- Many children still like to count 1–2, 3–4, rather than 2–4. Give them the experience of counting just in twos if they can. You may need to draw a new number line that misses out the odd numbers, or may not even have the marks in place (as in the line above from 10 onwards).

  What would be the next number you count, if we added two more counters? **12**.

  Do you see the digits 2, 4, 6, 8, 0 happening again? Where? **In 12, 14, 16, 18, 20**.

  What might happen after 20? **The same thing – 22, 24, 26, 28, 30 etc**.

- When counting in fives, you may need a different number line again, which highlights only the fives and tens, for example:

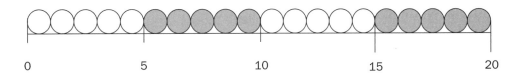

Beyond this, drawing a number line up to 100 would require some large paper. Alternatively, there are some number lines up to 100 with counters drawn on them and 100 squares also commercially available.

Later activities build on using the number line to add, subtract, multiply and divide.

Sequences of counters

This activity is designed to support children's under-standing of multiplication tables, helping them to count in twos, fives, tens, and other numbers as appropriate.

This will help children to:

- use odd and even numbers, and their links to the two times table

- consider multiples, such as three, five and ten, and others as appropriate

- (optional) predict later numbers in sequences, by considering factors.

You will need these resources:

- 50 counters, in two different colours

- some paper and a pencil.

The activity

- Get some counters in two different colours and begin by placing them in a sequence – for example, to highlight odd and even numbers:

What do you notice about this sequence of counters? **There is a light then dark counter**.

What colour do you think the next one will be? **Light**.

Can you carry on the sequence?

If we started counting the counters, what can you say about the tenth counter? **It will be dark**.

What other numbers will be represented by dark counters? **12, 14, 16 – even numbers**.

- Children may find it useful to separate the counters a little, and have the odd and even numbers written:

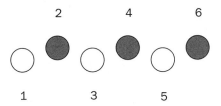

What numbers appear along the top? **Even**.

- Another visual scaffold would be to place the counters in a tower:

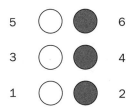

- As you say the numbers of counters, it is worth pointing out that the odd numbers have an odd one sticking up from the tower, but the even numbers are even (flat) on the top.

- Further sequences could explore other multiplication tables – for example, three times table:

What do you notice about this sequence of counters?

What colour do you think the next one will be? **Light**.

Can you carry on the sequence?

Is there anything special about the position of the dark counters? **Every third one**.

Will the tenth counter be dark or light? **Light** *How do you know?* **Because ten is not a third number/not in the three times table**.

What other numbers will be represented by dark counters? **3, 6, 9, 12, 15 etc.**

Can you make a sequence of your own? What can you tell me about your sequence?

- Repeat the activity for other times tables, such as the five times table:

The value of money

Some children are confused about the values of coins: coins come in different sizes, and these sizes are not related to value. So a 5p coin is smaller than a 2p coin; a 10p coin is larger and a different shape from a 20p coin. The only clue we have about how much a coin is worth is from the numeral written on it, but if is not understood how that numeral compares with others, then the value is not understood.

This activity will help children to:

- relate the value of coins to positions on a number line

- use the terms 'more than', 'less than', 'greatest', 'least', 'same value as'

- begin to find equivalent values – such as five lots of 2p is the same as 10p.

You will need these resources:

- 5 × 20p; 10 × 10p; 20 × 5p; 10 × 2p and 20 × 1p (a total of £3.40 in either real money or plastic coins)

- a metre ruler, or if not, a long and preferably large number line marked up to 100.

The activity

● Take one of each coin, and ask the child to place it in the right place on the number line. The example below goes up to 10p:

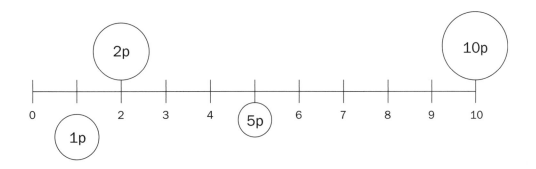

Which coin has the greatest value? **£1** (depending on which ones you have chosen to use).

Which coin has the least value? **1p**.

What can you say about the value of a 5p coin compared with a 10p coin? **It is less value/5p is not as much as 10p**.

Compare other coins in this way.

● Clear the ruler of coins.

Ask the child to count out five 1p coins and then place them along the number line at each number as set out below:

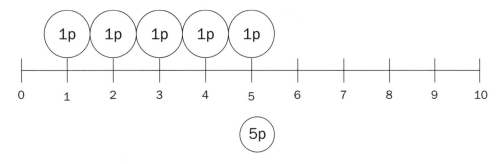

Where did you place the last 1p coin? **At the 5 mark**.

Is this the same place as one particular coin? **The 5p coin**.

Where would you reach if you placed ten 1p coins along the line? **The 10 mark, the same as the 10p coin**.

How many 1p coins would go as far as the 2p mark? **Two**.

How many 1p coins would go as far as the 20p mark (And so on)?

20p has the same value as twenty 1p coins. Are there any other connections you could make with 20p?

- Extend the task by using the number line to count in twos. For example, take five 2p coins, and ask the child to place them along the line.

    Where would you place the first 2p coin?

    Where would you place the second?

    Why are we missing one place out each time?

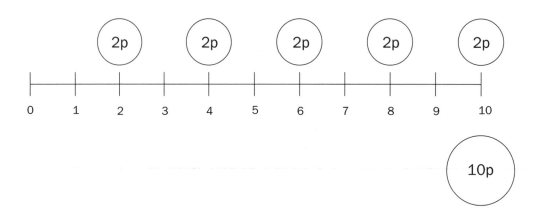

    Where do five 2p coins reach?

    What coin did we place at the '10' mark at first?

    What does that mean about the value of five 2p coins?

Counting small amounts of money

This is perhaps one of the simplest but most effective activities for reinforcing understanding about the value of numbers. However, the first objective here is for children to learn how to organise their counting: many children count in a haphazard way – for instance, in adding a series of 2p and 1p pieces, they may not think of separating the different coins and piling them into easy amounts such as 10p piles. Quite often they may try to count 1p, then 2p, then another 2p and so on. This may work for them with small numbers, but with larger numbers and a greater range of coins, errors will creep in.

This activity will help children to:

● count, organise and find totals of amounts of money

● count in twos, fives, tens and twenties, as appropriate.

You will need these resources:

● up to £5 worth of coins. You will need 10 × 20p; 10 × 10p; 20 × 5p; 30 × 2p and 40 × 1p. For extension tasks, bring in a couple of £1 coins and 4 or 5 × 50p pieces

● a number line may be used to help with counting in twos, fives etc.

The activity

- Start with using just two types of coin. The example below begins with 1p and 2p coins, but you could choose coins with higher denominations if the child is ready to count in fives or tens.

- Spread out five 2p coins and ten 1p coins on the table.

  How much money do we have here?

- Observe how the child works. Allow them to finish the task in their own way, and offer an answer, but if they do not attempt to organise the different coins into piles of 10p, then offer that way of working to them:

Here are the 2p coins in a pile:

Here are the 1p coins in a pile:

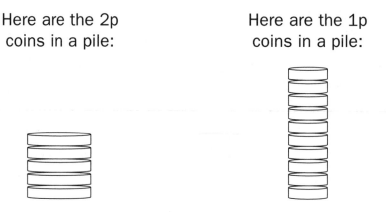

How much is in each pile? **10p in the twos and 10p worth of ones**.

How much do we have altogether? **10p and 10p makes 20p.**

Extensions

- There are different ways to develop these skills. The options given here can be taken in the order you choose, but they each have slightly different skills involved.

  Initially, the totals are multiples of 10p, but we can extend to other amounts after.

- Extend to using ten 2p coins and ten 1p coins, so that there are two piles of 2p coins – total 30p.

- Extend to other types of coins – for example:

ten 2p coins and two 5p coins – total 30p

twenty 1p coins and four 5p coins – total 40p

thirty 2p coins, eight 5p coins – total £1.

● Extend the number of types of coin – for example, three different types:

ten 2p, twenty 1p and four 5p coins – total 60p

six 5p coins, three 10p coins, two 20p coins – total £1.

● Extend to numbers of coins that do not pile up into ten exactly – for example:

twelve 2p coins and ten 1p coins – total 34p

five 5p coins and five 2p coins – total 35p.

● Extend to a random selection of coins.

Place value grids

As children become more familiar with counting, many need help to see the structure of the number system. Children may often see the hundred square to aid counting or place value, but this activity hides the numbers, and requires children to place the numbers in a part of the hundred square, so they have to think where the numbers go in order.

This activity will help children to:

● order numbers

● add 10 to or subtract 10 from a number and notice what happens to the tens and units.

You will need these resources:

● number cards (1–40 will be enough to start) and a blank grid of squares (such as the blank 5 cm grid provided in activity 20, 'Make a rectangle'. Parts of the grid can be photocopied and cut out; for example, you may wish to start with a smaller grid than the examples here

● a hundred square (as in activity 5, 'Journeys on a hundred square').

The activity

- Lay out some of the cards leaving gaps for the child to fill in, for example:

	22	23		25		27	28	29	
11		13	14		16	17			20
1	2	3		5	6			9	10

What number should we place between the three and the five? **4.**

What number goes above the 2? **12.** *How do you know?*

What number comes after the 29? **30.**

What can you say about all the numbers in the third column? **All end in 3 or have 3 in the units column.**

- Next reduce the part of the grid you are working with. Below, the grid is three across and four down. Place some of the cards in positions so that would be correct on a hundred square and ask the child to fill in the missing spaces.

	35	
	25	
14		16
		6

- You may wish to select only the cards that children will need to use, so that they do not have too many to choose from initially. Ask the child to complete the grid, and to explain why they placed the numbers in certain positions. The final grid should look like this:

34	35	36
24	25	26
14	15	16
4	5	6

- Some possible questions:

  What is the same about all the numbers in the second row down?

  What is the same about all the numbers in the second column? Any column?

  Why does the 14 go above the 4?

  Why is 26 below the 36?

  If I add 10 to 36 what number would I land on?

  Where should 7 be? Where should 33 be?

  Look at the 100 square – can you find this grid on it?

Extensions

- You could experiment with different-sized grids that you draw out yourself – or different-shaped grids, cut out from the original sheet – for example:

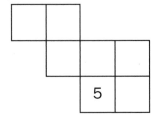

- Learners may also progress to completing a written grid, rather than continuing to use the cards. This will enable you to extend learning with the examples below.

- Sometimes, a learner's reasoning needs to be tested in situations that are less familiar. This grid may not appear on a normal 100 square, but it is still possible to complete, using the same rules as before:

29		
	20	

● If children are ready, then you could make up numbers over 100:

		123
	112	
101		

C. Developing images to support calculation

Children come to understand calculations in different ways, not necessarily through simply doing lots of sums, but also through physical activity including building shapes, comparing lengths or fitting pieces together. In this section, the activities focus on all four operations – addition, subtraction, multiplication and division – by using images such as number lines, rectangles and the hundred square, or physical equipment such as centimetre strips (or Cuisenaire rods).

It's important to realise that all calculations are effectively mental calculations – all we do when writing down sums is to record some thinking, usually so that we don't have to remember lots of numbers while completing the calculation. These activities fit into the principle that children should attempt to solve calculations mentally as a first resort, then use informal diagrams or notes to aid memory, and then we look at formal methods last of all.

The activities in this section enable children to sketch out their understanding with the support of diagrams. Although there is an accepted progression from addition, to subtraction, to multiplication and finally division (division uses both multiplication and subtraction skills), it is not intended that children do these one after the other: there may be a gap of years between activities – many children struggle with division even at secondary school.

The following activities are found in this section:

14. **Complements to ten** – using rod lengths to find pairs of numbers that sum to 10.

15. **Using number lines for addition** – a visual support for addition.

16. **Introducing number lines for subtraction: numbers up to ten** – exploring subtraction using number lines, carefully building the skills and increasing the size of the numbers used.

17. **Using number lines for subtraction: numbers over twenty**

18. **Using number lines for subtraction: difference is greater than ten**

19. **Giving change** – a structured shop activity.

20. **Make a rectangle** – linking multiples (and factors) with areas of rectangles.

21. **Factor walls** – understanding factors, using rods of different lengths.

22. **Using number lines for multiplication** – finding multiples of numbers, building on the number line image.

23. **Using number lines for division** – continuing the use of number lines, linking division with multiplication.

24. **Multiplying with cards and counters** – another image for multiplication.

Complements to ten

Perhaps without really knowing it, many of us use our ability to add two numbers up to 10 as a crucial step in lots of calculations, including addition, subtraction and giving change.

This activity will help children to:

● find pairs of numbers that sum to 10

● recognise connections and patterns in the numbers that sum to 10.

You will need these resources:

● Cuisenaire rods should be used for this activity. The different-coloured rods are fairly easy to handle, and are cut to different lengths of whole centimetres. However, the resource sheet in activity 8, 'Ten is greater than one', can be copied onto card and cut – albeit carefully – along the lines to make the exact sizes. One sheet of cards should be enough. Set out two of each length ready to use – that is, two each of 10 cm, 9 cm, 8 cm and so on to the 1 cm length.

The activity

● Take one of the largest (10 cm) lengths and place it on the table. Next to it, place the 8 cm length, and ask:

Can you choose another rod to fit into the space here?

● Children should be able to pick out the 2 cm rod, and fit it next to the 8 cm rod:

● Summarise by saying that the two rods 8 cm plus the 2 cm equals the 10 cm rod. You could write this down to show the child the numbers you are talking about.

● Put out the 10 cm rod again, and ask:

Can you find two other rods that fit together to make the same as the 10 cm rod?

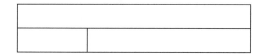

Which two numbers have you found fit together? **For example, 3 + 7.**

How shall we write this down? **For example, 3 + 7 = 10.**

● Try to find all the pairs – 1 + 9, 2 + 8, 3 + 7, 4 + 6, 5 + 5 and then 6 + 4, 7 + 3, 8 + 2, and 9 + 1.

● Make sure children make the connection that if they find that 3 + 7 = 10, then they can also tell us that 7 + 3 = 10. Perhaps demonstrate like this:

10cm	
3cm	7cm

7cm	3cm

Extension

● Although it is important for children to know the complements to ten, this technique could be used to find pairs of numbers that sum to any of the numbers, for example:

What pairs of numbers add up to 7? Use the rods to find out all the pairs you can.

These activities lend themselves well to making into 'games'; let children work in pairs and compete to see which pair select the most complements in a given time.

Using number lines for addition

When teaching addition or subtraction, children are sometimes presented too early with column sums to calculate, before developing a real understanding of the concepts. These number line activities help children build a visual support to understand the meaning of the four operations.

These activities help children:

- to relate adding with the number and visual representations.

You will need these resources:

- up to 100 counters – 50 of each of two colours

- you will also need to draw a number line where the scale is matched to the diameters of the counters, for example:

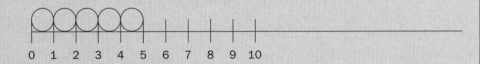

- It is likely that a number line marked all the way up to 20 or beyond will be needed. However, depending on the support the child needs, not all the numbers need to be marked in.

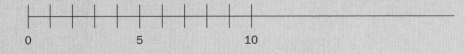

The activity

- Begin with the question:

  How can we use the number line to show 4 + 3?

- If the child is able to respond to this by moving the correct numbers of counters onto the number line and showing the result of 7, then move on to numbers with two digits.

- If not, move four counters onto the number line, one at a time, and ask the child to count, pointing to the numbers on the line as you go along.

  The sum was 4 + 3. What can we do with the other three counters?

- The child should be encouraged to move the counters in position, showing the result of 7.

- Try other sums. It may be necessary to keep the initial numbers to total 10 or less; for example, 8 + 2; 5 + 4; 6 + 2. However, also use the opportunity to build children's awareness of number bonds to 10, by introducing pairs such as 8 + 2, then 2 + 8, 7 + 3, then 3 + 7 etc. (note activity 14, 'Complements to ten').

- Next, go over the 10:

  Can you try other sums – for example, 8 + 5? 9 + 7?

  How about 18 + 5? What do you notice, compared with 8 + 5?

Extensions

- Move on to addition using the number line but without the counters. This can be extended to any size numbers eventually.

  For example, on a number line up to 100: *What is 68 + 5?*

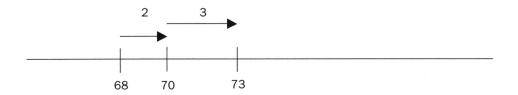

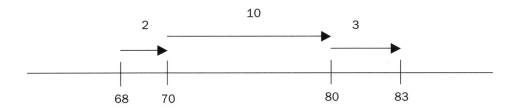

- Children may find 5 easy to break up into 2 + 3, therefore using 70 as a stepping-stone. However, they may experience difficulties when adding two two-digit numbers:

  How about 68 + 15?

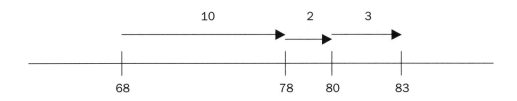

- These difficulties may be overcome by going back to using 15 counters, and then using two of them to get to 70, leaving 13. Then use 10 to get to 80, leaving 3 to make 83.

- However, some children prefer to add the tens first:

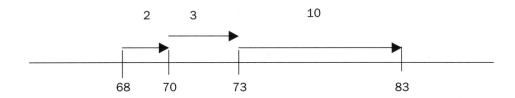

- Other children prefer to add the units first:

- The key is to build children's confidence in their own methods.

Introducing number lines for subtraction: numbers up to ten

There are at least two ways of showing subtractions on number lines: one is to start with the largest number, and physically take away the smaller value (counting down); the other is to focus on the *difference* between the two numbers. Many children find looking for differences easier to understand and to handle, because it uses addition from the smaller to the larger number.

Using the number line allows for careful progression, from small numbers, then moving on to two-digit or three-digit numbers, including decimals. The progression will be explored in the subtraction activities 17 and 18.

This activity will help children to:

- develop a visual picture of subtraction

- link subtraction with addition and use the term 'difference'

- subtract numbers up to 10.

You will need these resources:

- up to 20 counters

- number lines where the scale is matched to the diameters of the counters, for example:

The activity

- Begin with the question: *How can we use the number line to show 8 – 5?*

- It might be natural to start with the eight counters on the line and then take five away (below), leaving three.

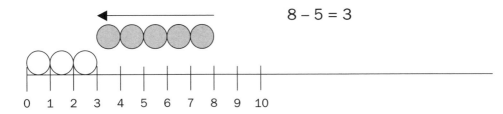

$$8 - 5 = 3$$

- However, the method below asks children to find the 8 on the number line using one colour, and then go back to find 5 on the number line, take those counters away and count on from the five to the eight:

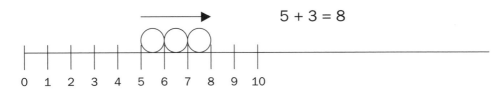

$$5 + 3 = 8$$

- Children may need to count the individual numbers between five and eight, as in 1, 2, 3; or they may state the answer 3 just by looking at the jump.

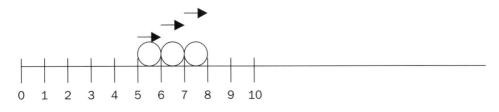

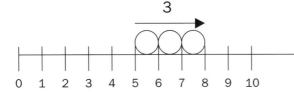

Other questions

How can we use the number line to show 9 – 4?

- Try with a range of calculations – up to 10, for example, 7 – 3; 10 – 2 etc.

Using number lines for subtraction: numbers over twenty

Having introduced number lines for subtraction with the previous activity, this activity builds a progression for children. The progression will have two aspects: making the numbers more complex (perhaps working with larger numbers or decimals), and/or removing some of the scaffolding or support (taking away the counters and/or the markings on the number line, so that children create their own).

This activity will help children to:

- subtract single-digit numbers from two-digit numbers by counting on

- use the number lines in a more efficient way to subtract

- identify patterns in subtractions – for example, where 14 – 8 gives the same result as 24 – 18

- subtract two-digit numbers from other two-digit numbers, where the difference is less than 10.

You will need these resources:

- 20 counters, 10 each of two different colours

- a range of number lines up to the numbers appropriate for the child – perhaps up to 100. Depending on the needs of the child, you may need some that are

a) Fully numbered – where you indicate all the whole numbers:

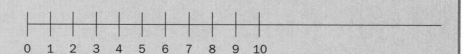

b) where you place all the relevant markings but only a selection of the numbers (as on a ruler), for example:

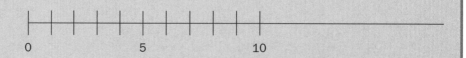

c) A bit more open, with some numbers and some markings:

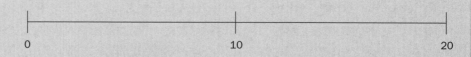

d) Completely open – this is where the child chooses for themselves how to mark. All you may need to do is to draw a straight line as a prompt.

The activity

● First, bridge over 10: How can we use the number line to show 14 – 8?

● Bridging over 10 is often approached by counting in two jumps; for example, here from 8 to 10, then 10 to 14.

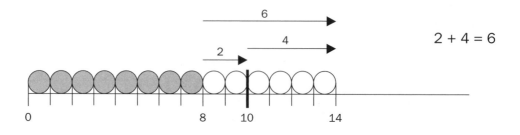

2 + 4 = 6

- Second, try just using the image of number lines without counters; for example, *How can we use the number line to show 15 − 7?*

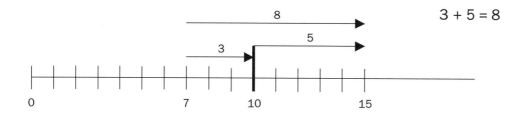

$3 + 5 = 8$

- Use the first example (14 − 8) and build on it, for example:

    How can we use the number line to show 24 − 18?

    Why is the answer the same as for 14 − 8? **The difference is the same**.

    What if we tried 34 − 28? **The difference is the same**.

    Can you give me another pair of numbers with the same difference? **44 − 38, 54 − 48 etc.**

- Children may need the support of marked and numbered lines, but they could try to progress towards open lines, for example:

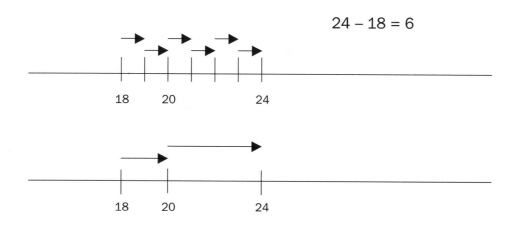

$24 − 18 = 6$

Extensions

- Try building this idea from similar examples; for example, 16 − 7, 26 − 17, 36 − 27; 13 − 5, 23 − 15 etc.

Using number lines for subtraction: difference is greater than ten

The power of this visual representation of subtraction lies in the progression to larger numbers or decimals.

This activity will help children to:

- subtract two-digit numbers from other two-digit numbers, where the difference is greater than 10.

You will need these resources:

- a range of number lines, as shown in the previous activity.

The activity

- For example, let's look at the subtraction 65 – 37.

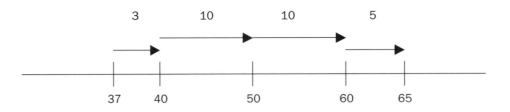

- Children may need to count in single tens initially.

  What numbers do we add to get our answer? The calculation is 10 + 10 + 5 + 3 = 28.

What if you added these numbers another way? Children may order the numbers in any way they wish to make the sum easier to handle.

What number could we use instead of 10 + 10? Children may be encouraged to combine the tens:

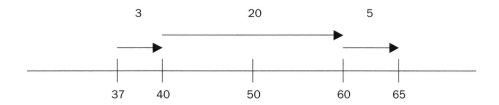

Consolidation

● It is worth helping children to practise placing numbers on the line for themselves. Have ready a range of number lines.

> *Give me a number less than 10. Can you place it on a number line?*

> *Give me a number less than 20. Can you place it on a number line?*

● Once children are familiar with this, move on to using this skill for themselves to subtract two two-digit numbers.

> *Give me any two-digit number. Can you place it on a number line?*

> *Give me another two-digit number, and place it on the number line.*

> *Can you find the difference between your two numbers?*

Extension

● This technique works equally well for hundreds, for example, 650 − 370 = 280.

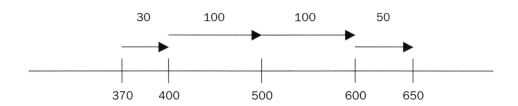

● And for decimals; for example, $6.5 - 3.7 = 2.8$

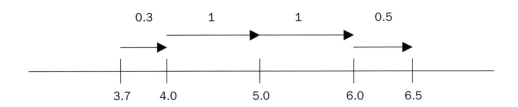

Giving change

'Shopkeeper maths' offers us a realistic and practical way to handle numbers that people do not regularly experience nowadays. Giving change relates addition directly with subtraction, because we use counting on to identify how much change is needed. However, it is also important to build the skill of choosing the least number of coins needed for the change. We shall have to develop this skill gradually through the activity.

Some children do not see that when you shop, there is a balancing act– between you parting with an amount of money, and the shopkeeper giving you an item and a smaller amount of money to equal the amount you have given. The activity will attempt to help children see this balancing going on.

This activity will help children to:

- understand what giving change means

- count on from a given number

- relate subtraction with the idea of difference, and counting on

- minimise the number of coins used in giving change

- relate numbers to positions on a number line.

You will need these resources:

- a £1 coin; 1 × 50p; 5 × 20p; 10 × 10p; 2 × 5p; 10 × 2p and 20 × 1p

- a few objects to pretend to buy – for example, a book, pencil, notepad, chocolate bar, toy, fruit

- a metre ruler or a number line – adapted for each situation – if you are giving change to £1, it needs to go up to 100.

The activity

- Label the items with prices (or agree them with the child as you go along). These can change during the activity, and your starting point depends on the current level of the child's understanding, for example, for some children, keep the numbers less than 10p, for others you may be considering giving change from 20p, 50p or £1 (or more). The two of you should play different roles in the shop – you act as the shopper, and the child acts as the shopkeeper. Give the child most of the money, but you keep some specific coins to use – 1 × 10p, 1 × 20p, 1 × 50p and the £1 coin. You pretend to buy any of the items.

- For example, pick up an item (say a toy car) that is worth 8p.

  How much money do I have to give you to buy the tractor? **8p**.

  Look at my coins – do I have 8p? **No**. *What can I do?*

  If I give you this 10p coin, that's a bit more than you are giving me. So you have to give me a little more to equal 10p. How much more?

- To make the balancing clearer, it may be useful to place the car and the 2p on one side, and the 10p you are giving on the other:

  Here is my 10p and here is the car, which is the same as 8p. To make this fair, you have to give me 2p to go with the 8p to match my 10p.

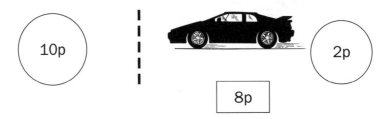

- Alternatively, or in addition, it may be useful to use a number line to point to the numbers and show the difference.

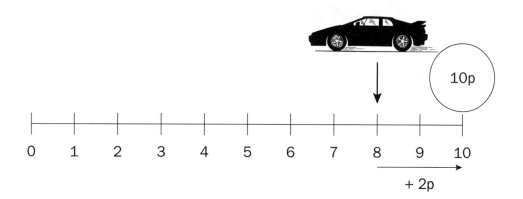

- Children may need to count 1p and 1p to make 2p altogether. *How much change will you give me?* **2p**.

- This next question is only suitable if the child is ready to consider the smallest number of coins possible.

  Can you give me the change in just one coin? **A 2p coin**.

Extensions

- Change the value of the car to other amounts less than 10p. Then reinforce by working with values such as 17p or 18p, giving the child the 20p coin. You can then build up to values such as 47p and 48p, working with the 50p coin, and similarly 97p and 98p with the £1 coin. Consider soon the object being worth 5p, and giving a 10p coin to pay for it, and ensure that the child makes the step to giving a 5p coin as change.

- Next, you could consider the value of the object being 10p, and paying for it with a 20p coin. This will bring in the use of the 10p coin in the change, and you can then progress to amounts such as 9p, then 8p and 7p for the object, paying for it with a 20p coin. Then, amounts up to £1 can be handled.

Make a rectangle

This is a fundamental concept in understanding number, where we match the idea of an area of a rectangle – the space the rectangle takes up – with multiples (times tables). The idea enables learners to progress through a variety of mathematical concepts: counting in twos, threes, etc., exploring factors of numbers; linking multiplication and division. Older learners can also use this idea when multiplying large numbers, or even expanding brackets in algebra. This activity attempts to make these links for younger learners or those who may have difficulties understanding what multiplication means. To emphasise the links, this activity builds on the ideas in activity 2, 'Arrays of counters' and later you may consider the ideas in 21, 'Factor walls' to take it even further.

This activity will help children to:

- build rectangles using square cards, and find the links between their areas and the widths and lengths of the rectangles

- identify the factors of certain numbers, such as 6, 8, 9, 10 and 12

- meet numbers that only have two factors, when they find they can only make one rectangle.

You will need these resources:

- about 40 card squares using the 5 cm squares template on page 71

- a set of the squared number cards.

The activity

- Ask the children to count out six square cards. The idea is that children make a rectangle using all the squares. Children should end up with either one of the two possibilities – a 2 × 3 or a 6 × 1 rectangle.

  Can you make a rectangle using all of these squares? **Yes.**

  How much space is taken up by the rectangle? **Six squares.**

  How many different rectangles can you make? **Two different ones.**

- State that the side lengths (1 and 6, 2 and 3) are all *factors* of 6.

- Use the number cards to highlight counting in twos or threes:

Three twos   Two threes:

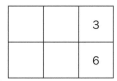

- You can now choose which numbers of squares to use to build other rectangles; for example, 8 and 10:

  What happens when you use eight squares to make a rectangle? **Two rectangles – 1 × 8 and 2 × 4.**

● Again, bringing in the number cards and perhaps slightly separating the squares can highlight the fact that 8 can be made from four twos or two fours:

Can you make two rectangles with ten squares? **Yes – 1 × 10 and 2 × 5.**

Extensions

Can you always make two rectangles?

● To answer this, try with various numbers of squares; for example, 5, 7, 9 and 12.

How many rectangles can you make with five squares? **We can only make one rectangle: a 1 × 5.**

How many rectangles can you make with seven squares? **Again, we can only make one rectangle: a 1 × 7.**

How many rectangles can you make with nine squares? **We get a 1 × 9 rectangle, and we get a square – 3 × 3.**

How many rectangles can you make with 12 squares? **We get a 1 × 12, a 2 × 6 and a third rectangle – a 3 × 4.**

Further extensions

● Try with larger numbers; for example, 15, 16 and 24 give interesting results. Using 15 cannot make a rectangle with one side of length two, but can make a side of length three (3 × 5); 16 produces another square (like nine), and 24 has four different rectangles (1 × 24, 2 × 12, 3 × 8 and 4 × 6).

● Children may wish to record systematically all the possible rectangles that can be made from different numbers of square cards. They may wish to draw their results on squared paper, or put the results in some kind of table.

Number cards

1	2	3
4	5	6
7	8	9
10	11	12

13	14	15
16	17	18
19	20	21
22	23	24

25	26	27
28	29	30
31	32	33
34	35	36

37	38	39
40	41	42
43	44	45
46	47	48

Factor walls

Here is an activity that enables children to find factors of numbers. It could also be used to identify prime numbers, and is a good activity to do perhaps alongside activity 20, 'Make a rectangle', because offering the two activities close together will help children to understand factors in slightly different physical situations.

The activity should help children to:

● find factors of numbers up to 10

● identify prime numbers

● explain why some numbers are or are not factors of another.

You will need these resources:

● Cuisenaire rods should be used for this activity. However, a resource sheet with all the lengths from 1 cm to 10 cm is provided in activity 8, 'Ten is greater than one', which can be copied onto card and cut out.

The activity

● Take the largest (10 cm) rod, and below it line up some 2 cm rods: five will be needed.

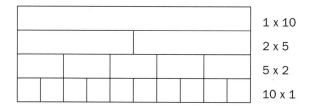

	10cm
	5 x 2cm

What can you say about any of the rods? How long are the rods?

We know 5 × 2 = 10. Are there any other rods that would fit exactly under the 10 cm rod?

● In each row, the rods have to be the same colour/pattern/length. We are looking for factors of 10, not complements. A factor wall for the 10 cm rod would look like this:

	1 x 10
	2 x 5
	5 x 2
	10 x 1

● Children might quickly identify that the 1 cm (unit) rod will fit. They may also find that two of the 5 cm rods will fit. It is worth allowing them to try all the rods, finding:

What happens if you try some of the 3 cm rods? Do they fit exactly? Do you know why not?

The numbers we have found (1, 2, 5 and 10) are all factors of ten.

Is 3 a factor of 10? **No, because it did not fit exactly**.

● It is best to demonstrate this, perhaps as shown below:

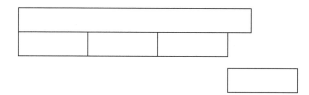

● Three threes reach nearly as far as the 10 cm, but not quite. Another 3 would be too big. So 3 is not a factor of 10.

Are any other numbers factors of 10? **No**.

● Now start with the 9 cm rod.

Can you build the factor wall for this rod?

factor walls

77

Why does the 2 cm rod not fit this time? **2 is not a factor of 9; there is one space/square left over; 5 × 2 makes 10, which is one square/space too long**.

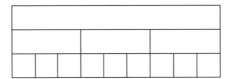

Extension activities

- You may wish for the children to build the factor walls for all the rods.

  Which rods can be built only with themselves and the 1 cm rods?

- Some (the 2, 3, 5, 7 cm rods) will only be built of the single 1 cm rods alongside them. These numbers are the prime numbers.

Using number lines for multiplication

This activity extends the number line ideas used in addition and builds directly on the earlier activities using number lines. It gives children a different way of looking at multiplication, using the idea of repeated addition. This activity can be considered as part of a set along with activity 20, 'Make a rectangle', and activity 24, 'Multiplying with cards and counters'.

This activity will help children to:

● count in twos, threes, etc. up to tens

● find multiples of numbers, by matching the result against a number line or metre ruler.

You will need these resources:

● up to 30 counters in at least two different colours

● a number line up to 30 where the scale is matched to the diameters of the counters, for example:

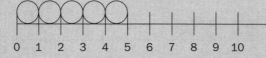

0 1 2 3 4 5 6 7 8 9 10

Alternatively, and especially for tackling the multiples of 7, 8 and 9, it may be better to use:

> ● strips of coloured card cut to various whole centimetre lengths – or use the resource sheet provided in activity 8, 'Ten is greater than one'. Alternatively, Cuisenaire rods are ideal, as they are already cut to different lengths
>
> ● a metre rule, or a number line that is measured in centimetres.

The activity

● Your choice of the multiples to work with will depend on the needs of the child. The example below begins with working in threes, but could equally apply to any number up to 6.

● Using two different colours, the threes can be highlighted:

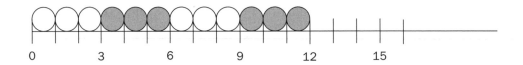

What numbers do we reach after every three counters? **3, 6, 9, 12 etc**.

Can you count on without the counters? Where would the next three counters reach? **15**.

Extension/progression

● For some children, it may be useful to work on pairs of multiplication tables together. For example, alongside the three times table, you could have another number line showing the six times table. This will give an opportunity for children to make links between tables.

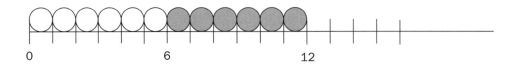

Which numbers are in the six times table? **6, 12, 18 etc**.

Where will the next six counters reach?

What numbers are the same in the three times table? **6, 12, 18 etc**.

What type of number is missing? **The odd ones**.

- Children's understanding could also progress by removing the support of the counters, and using the number line itself to count on in the multiplication table.

For example:

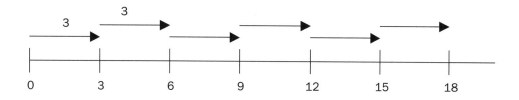

- Once children are comfortable with this technique, it can be used for the harder multiplication tables – 7, 8 or 9.

Alternative resources

- You could use the centimetre strips (in the resources) or Cuisenaire rods against a metre rule to help children recognise how the multiplication tables build up. Again these may be especially useful for the harder multiplication tables.

For example, the 8 cm rod could be used against a metre rule as below:

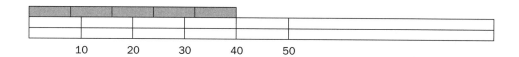

If we put one end on zero, where does this rod reach? **8 cm**.

How long are two 8 cm rods? **16 cm**.

What numbers do the 8 cm rods reach? **8, 16, 24, 32, 40 etc**.

Where will the next rod reach on the metre rule? **48**.

How many 8 cm rods do you need to reach 40 cm? **5**.

How many 8 cm rods would you need to reach 80 cm? **10**.

Using number lines for division

Division is often considered to be the hardest of the four operations to calculate accurately and consistently. Our methods for solving division problems usually combine multiplication techniques with subtraction, and both these have to be reasonably secure or many errors creep in.

Another technique for solving division problems uses repeated subtraction, which can be long-winded unless another skill – using estimation – is employed. We find too many children struggling with division calculations well into their secondary school years, often because they are not clear about what division means, or they do not apply the above skills to solve the problems.

This activity will help children to:

- make explicit the links between multiplication and division

- reinforce their use of multiplication tables

- use the number line image alongside existing ways of looking at sharing and grouping.

You will need these resources:

- up to 60 counters – perhaps 30 each of two different colours

- number lines drawn to match the size of the counters – as with the previous number line activities

- coins (for example, 30 pennies and six 5p pieces, and three 10p pieces) for the money problem.

The activity

- Division has two contexts that can be best described as sharing and grouping. The answer (**4**) each time in the example below is the same, even though the physical representation of the problem is different.

  Sharing is for example 20 biscuits shared by 5 people – *how many biscuits does each have?* **4**.

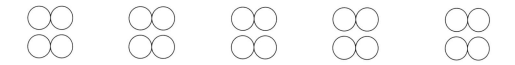

  Grouping might be exemplified as the same 20 biscuits packed in mini-packs of 5 – *how many mini-packs are made?* **4**.

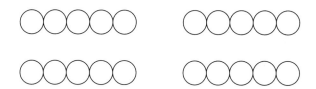

- The number line method uses the idea of grouping, because it will use the multiplication table – in this case the five times table – to solve the problem. Moving forwards on the number line from zero revisits and reinforces multiplication facts – as with the five times table – 1 × 5 = 5, 2 × 5 = 10 and so on. So with *grouping* in the biscuits problem:

Number of biscuits

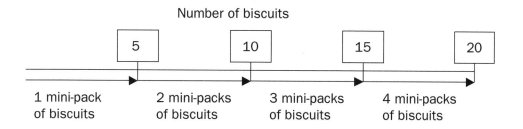

● Here is another problem. The different representations are not offered as a choice, but as a range of perspectives of the same problem – if children have experience of all these representations, they can then begin to choose how they will solve other problems.

If you have 30 pennies and you want to change them into 5p pieces, how many 5p pieces would you have?

Represented as counters/coins in groups – six groups of 5:

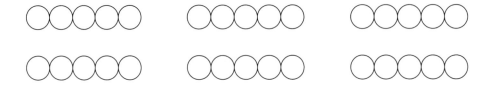

Represented as counters/coins on the number line:

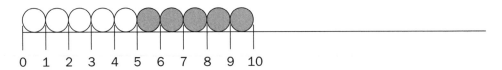

Represented on the number line without counters or coins:

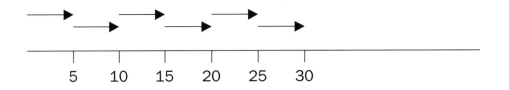

● Try to set a number of problems for the child to look at in these different ways, for example:

48 eggs to be placed in boxes of 6 – how many boxes are needed?

60 Christmas cards in packs of 10 – how many packs?

24 mugs in boxes of 4 – how many boxes are needed?

16 socks – how many pairs?

Multiplying with cards and counters

This is a way of helping children understand what multiplication means, by using cards and counters.

The activity should help children to:

● see multiplication as repeated addition

● become familiar with the language associated with multiplication

● look for multiplicative links between numbers.

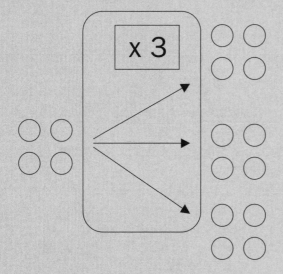

The resources you need are:

● the multiplication cards are printed on pages 88–89

● up to 50 counters.

Activity 1

● Place a number of counters on the left – for example, 4 – then place a multiplication card next to it. Ask the child to place the correct number of counters on the right of the card, using the arrows to show how the original number is multiplied (as in the diagram above).

Children should become familiar with the range of language associated with multiplication, because they will meet the range on many occasions. We should therefore be concerned that they can be flexible with the language:

What are three fours?

What are three times four?

What is four multiplied by three?

What are three lots of four?

4 × 3 = ?

This initial activity can be repeated with any suitable numbers of counters, and different multiplier cards.

Activity 2

● This activity turns the question around, so that children focus on the multiplicative relationship between numbers.

● Place, for example, three counters on the left, and six on the right, as below.

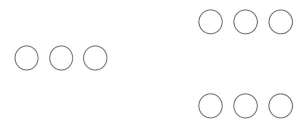

Which card goes in the middle? **The 'times 2' card**.

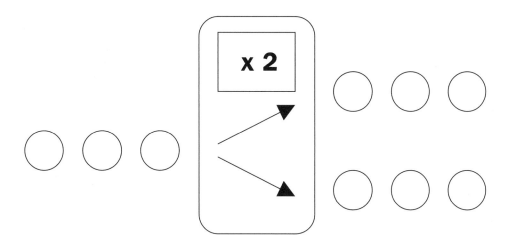

What are we multiplying by 2? **The three counters**.

What is the result of three counters times two? **Six counters**.

- Repeat for several pairs of numbers, for example, 3 and 15, 2 and 8.

- Children can set their own questions, but may need to draw out their own cards; for example, if they choose two counters one side and 12 the other, they will need to make up a '✕ 6' card.

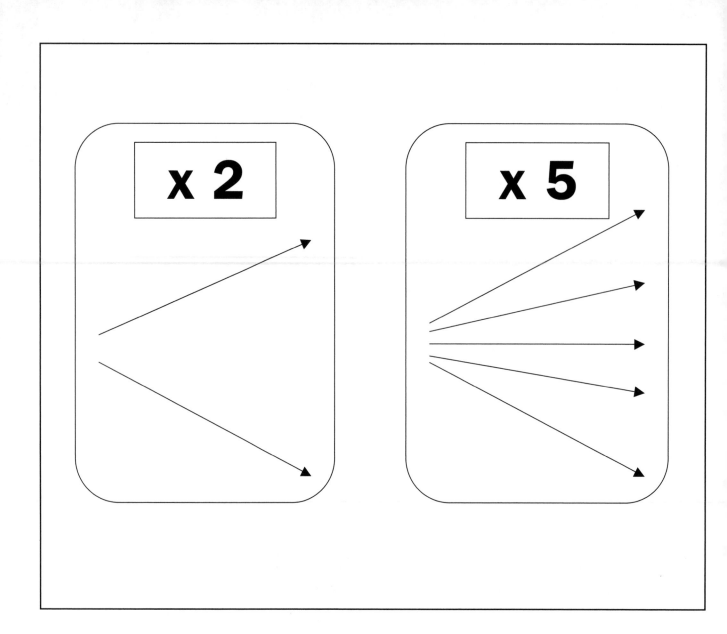

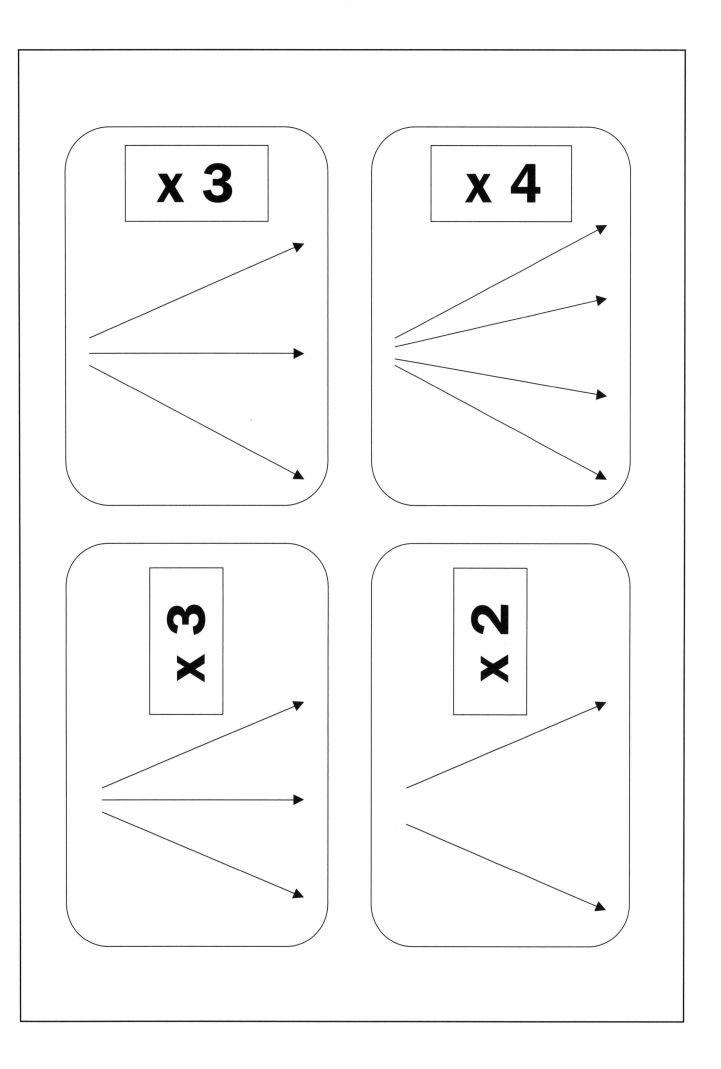

D. Organising thinking to aid calculation

Children who struggle with calculating sometimes need help in seeing how numbers and the four operations are connected, and how they can use these connections to make the calculations easier. (We can compare this to driving – knowing the road system and how to use alternative routes to get to a destination.) These activities help children to see these techniques and to use them effectively to understand calculations.

The following activities are found in this section:

25. **Reordering to find complements** – reordering addition (and subtraction) sums so that pairs of numbers that sum to 10 are close together to aid calculation.

26. **Partitioning** – separating the tens and units in addition and subtraction sums, to calculate with the tens and then the units, and then combining the results.

27. **Piecing together multiplication tables** – making links in multiplication tables clear, to help calculate other parts of the tables

Reordering to find complements

It is important for learners to establish how they can solve problems with numbers. There are various ways of making calculations easier: for addition, one technique is to use reordering to link numbers that sum to 10.

This activity will help children to:

- add several numbers together

- make complements to 10

- reorder numbers and use this technique to make addition of several numbers easier.

The extension will use complements to 20.

You will need these resources:

- a set of number cards 1–10 from the set given with activity 20, 'Make a rectangle'.

Preparatory activity

- Use four carefully selected cards – for example, 3, 4, 6, 7, selected in such a way as to have two pairs of numbers that add up to ten (3 and 7, 4 and 6). Spread them out on the table, and ask:

  What is the total if you added all the cards?

- Encourage children to pair off the cards to give the sum of 10 and 10 making 20.

Main activity

- Spread all the cards face up on the table.

  Can you find an easy way to add all the numbers on the cards together?

- Many children will count, 1 + 2 + 3 etc. Some will succeed with this. However, an easier way is to move the cards into pairs that sum to 10: the 9 + 1, 8 + 2 and so on.

- If children have not seen this, then help them by asking:

  What if we added these two cards? (For example, show them the 9 + 1) **We get 10**.

  Are there any other pairs which sum to 10? **8 + 2, 7 + 3, 6 + 4 and the 5 we leave on its own**.

  Count in tens, what is the total? **50 and the 5 makes 55**.

Extension activity: finding complements to 20

- Select some of the 1–20 cards; for example, 1, 19, 17, 3 and ask for the sum of these. Again encourage pairing this time to 20: 19 + 1, 17 + 3. It may be easier to start with numbers 1, 2, 3 and their complements 17, 18, 19 rather than using 8 with 12, where there is a lot to count on.

  What is the total of all the 1–20 cards? Can we still pair the cards to help us?

Partitioning

This is another essential skill in simplifying mental calculations – many of us separate the tens and the units when adding pairs of 2-digit numbers (and some do for subtracting). At the heart of this is an understanding that the result of adding the units in a pair of numbers is not affected by what happens with the tens: for example, 4 + 5 are 9, and 14 + 25 are 39 – the 9 remains consistent. This activity attempts to make this clear to children.

This activity will help children to:

● partition two-digit numbers

● add numbers, by partitioning the tens and units

● discuss the effect of place value in addition sums.

You will need these resources:

● pencil and paper.

Optional:

● counters

● 12 × 10p and at least 20 × 1p coins

● a hundred square (see activity 5, 'Journeys on a hundred square')

- Cuisenaire rod set – or the printed sheet of lengths in activity 8, 'Ten is greater than one'

- number line or metre rule.

The activity

- The first thing to establish is for children to be aware of the effect of changing the tens in a calculation. For example, start with:

  What is the result of 4 + 3? **7**.

- (Use whatever resources are necessary to establish the solution; for example, physical resources such as counters or penny coins, or representative visual resources such as a number line or a metre ruler marked in centimetres.)

  What is the result of 14 + 3? **17**.

- The focus is on the fact that the tens digit makes no difference to what happens with the units.

- If using coins, have the 4p and 3p as before. This time use a 10p piece alongside the 4p to show the 14p.

- Encourage the child to start counting from the 10p, then count on the 4 and then the 3 to get to the 17p. Write out the two sums (4 + 3 = 7, and 14 + 3 = 17), and then point out that the 7 part is still the same, the only difference is in the 10.

- The hundred square can be used with counters:

91	92	93	94	95	96	97	98	99	100
81	82	83	84	85	86	87	88	89	90
71	72	73	74	75	76	77	78	79	80
61	62	63	64	65	66	67	68	69	70
51	52	53	54	55	56	57	58	59	60
41	42	43	44	45	46	47	48	49	50
31	32	33	34	35	36	37	38	39	40
21	22	23	24	25	26	27	28	29	30
11	12	13	14	15	16	17	18	19	20
1	2	3	4	5	6	7	8	9	10

This square shows $4 + 3 = 7$.

- Then point to the 14, and ask the child to add on three counters – finishing at 17.

- You can extend these questions to 24 + 3, 34 + 3, or 104 + 3, or 224 + 3 or 4 + 13, 24 + 13 etc. depending on how the child is coping with these ideas. Keep using the physical resources to ensure understanding.

Extension and consolidation

- These ideas can be reinforced through exploring different pairs of units; for example, 2 + 6, 4 + 5, 1 + 8, then going on to change the tens digit – 12 + 6, 22 + 16 etc.

Adding a pair of two-digit numbers

- If, for example, 24 + 35 is represented using 10p pieces for both the 20 and the 30, and single coins for the units, then children can be encouraged to count the values separately: 20 + 30 = 50, 4 + 5 = 9, 50 + 9 = 59. Children may need to count from 50 with the 9 to confirm this, but certainly encourage them to start from 50 (and not from 1 all the way to 59).

- *Try to add 34p and 56p. What can you do to make the calculation easier?* **Count the units together (10), and count the tens together (80), and add these two numbers to make 90.**

- An extension to this would be to try adding three numbers, such as 13 + 12 + 24, by adding the tens and the units separately, then combining them.

Piecing together multiplication tables

Children who can't confidently use their times tables may find that the only strategy they can use is to add on the number each time – so, for example, they construct the six times table by starting with 6, then add on 6 to make 12 and so on. This activity encourages children to look at a range of ways of building the tables, so that although they may not be able to immediately recall them, they can at least get there by using doubling and halving and adding on.

This activity will help children to:

- make and use links between numbers to calculate multiplication tables.

You will need these resources:

- pencil and paper

- highlighter pens to show the different doubles connections.

The activity

- It may be useful to demonstrate the links in multiplication tables with an easy table that they know, such as the two or the five times table.

- Write out the table, and *together* write out the answers.

$1 \times 5 = 5$

$2 \times 5 = 10$

$3 \times 5 = 15$

$\cdots$

$10 \times 5 = 50$

- Next, point to the $2 \times 5 = 10$, and state that the answer 10 is double $1 \times 5 = 5$.

$1 \times 5 = 5$
$2 \times 5 = 10$ } Double

What other doubles can you see in the table?

- Encourage the child to look for as many doubles as they can.

- Point out for example that 4×5 is double 2×5, so 20 is double 10.

```
                        1 x 5 = 5        10 is double 5
                        2 x 5 = 10
                        3 x 5 = 15       20 is double 10
                        4 x 5 = 20
30 is double 15         5 x 5 = 25
                        6 x 5 = 30       40 is double 20
                        7 x 5 = 35
50 is double 25         8 x 5 = 40
                        9 x 5 = 45
                        10 x 5 = 50
```

- Next, choose whatever multiplication table is appropriate for the child to work on. The example below looks at the six times table, but the ideas can be used for any of them. Write out the table as below, without answers:

$1 \times 6 =$

$2 \times 6 =$

. . .

$9 \times 6 =$

$10 \times 6 = 60$

● This is where we use the idea of doubles and halves. For example, if we know that 10×6 is 60, then we use the fact that 5×6 is half that.

$5 \times 6 = 30$

$10 \times 6 = 60$

● Build up all the other numbers that can be made by doubling or halving. Then build up the other results; for example, adding 6 to 12 to get $3 \times 6 = 18$; then use the doubling again to get $6 \times 6 = 36$.

$3 \times 6 = 18$

$6 \times 6 = 36$

● Children could find 9×6 by either adding on 6 to the result for 8×6, so $48 + 6 = 54$, or they can look at $10 \times 6 = 60$, and so we take 6 away, again giving 54.

● Indeed, it is best to use both techniques – addition and subtraction – to confirm the answers, to demonstrate that checking our work is an important attribute.

● There are a number of ways to find 7×6 – probably through adding on 6 from $6 \times 6 = 36$, but also checking by subtracting 6 from 8×6.

E. Time

Learning to tell the time combines a number of skills and ideas. It relates two units (hours and minutes) to specific positions around a wheel; it relates the five times table to the same positions as the numbers 1 to 12; it uses language (past and to the hour) that depend on having visualised the minute hand passing the half-hour; it uses images of fractions (quarter and half hours) within the language we use and it can be presented in both analogue and digital forms, and 12-hour and 24-hour forms. That is quite a lot to handle, so the activities offered here focus on two of these aspects: relating the positions of numbers of both hours and minutes around the clock face, and connecting the language of past and to the hour with fraction shapes.

The following activities are found in this section:

28. **Wheels of time** – recognising the positions of the numbers 1 to 12 on an analogue clock and linking the five times table to the minutes past the hour.

29. **Fractions of time** – helping to recognise the minutes past or the minutes to the hour, by using shapes that are fractions of a circle.

Wheels of time

Although this activity is presented as a diagram, it could just as effectively be undertaken by having 12 people placed in a circle in the hour positions, being given the relevant number cards.

This activity will help children to:

- relate numbers to the positions on an analogue clock

- use the five times table and relate it to minutes.

You will need these resources:

- a wheel of spokes like the ones in the diagrams below (in resource sheet on page 104)

- cards marked with the numbers 1–12

- another set of cards with the numbers 5–60 in fives (in the resource sheet on page 105)

- (optional) a set of cards with the five times table written on them; for example, $2 \times 5 = 10$ as indicated below (not included)

- a real, clear analogue clock is also needed.

The activity

● Using a blank set of spokes and a real clock, ask the child to place the cards 1 to 12 around the spokes in the correct positions in order.

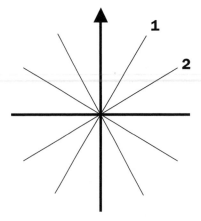

● Begin again, shuffling the number cards, and then turning them up one by one, asking the child to place them correctly. For example, the cards could turn up 9 first, then 6, and so on.

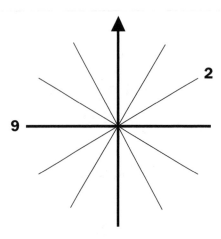

● Then use the 5–60 cards, and ask the child to place them in order around the clock and to say the numbers out loud at the same time.

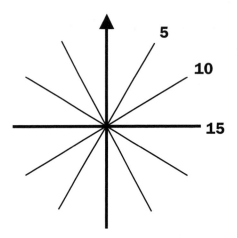

- Count the minutes on the real clock to show where the 5, 10, 15 etc. minutes are placed. Then develop the understanding by shuffling these cards, and asking the child to place them correctly, in whatever order they turn up, for example, '*Where do we read 25 minutes to? 35 minutes?*'

- It may be useful to count round the clock in fives with the child as they place the cards. If necessary, have a set of cards showing the five times table written out to prompt their thinking:

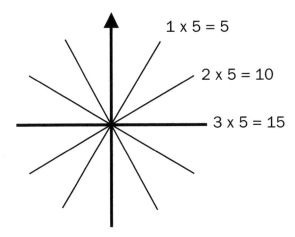

1 x 5 = 5

2 x 5 = 10

3 x 5 = 15

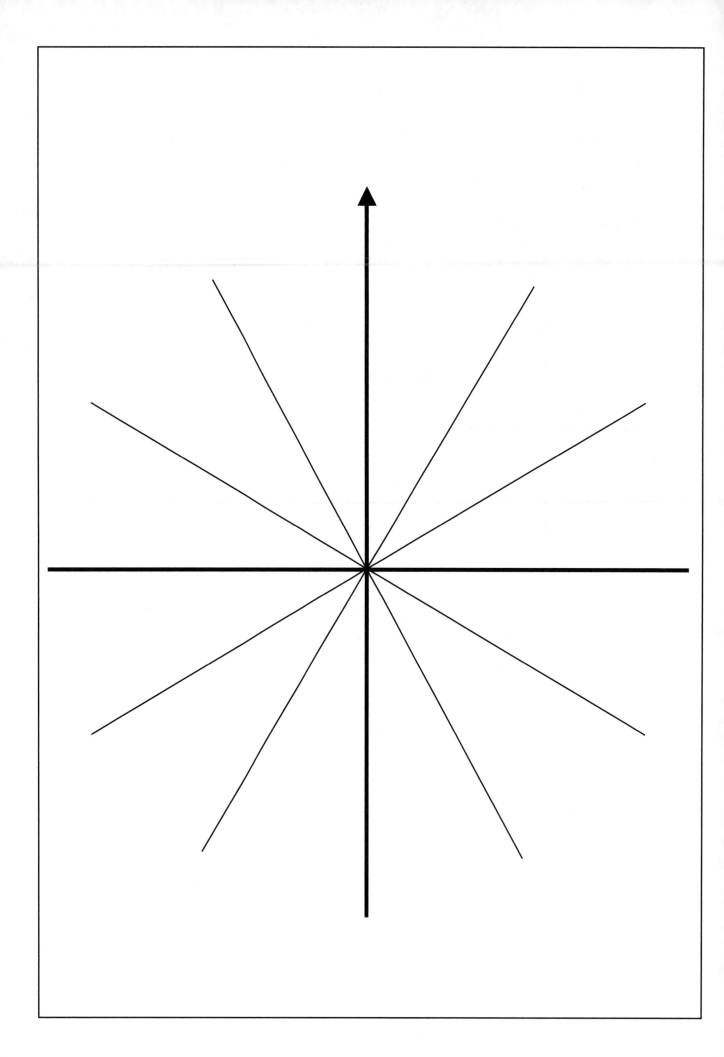

5	10	15
20	25	30
35	40	45
50	55	60

Fractions of time

This is a simple activity to help children build a picture of the parts of the hour that we use to tell the time. Many people relate the terms – for example '5 past the hour' and '20 to the hour' – to shapes or fractions of a circle, rather than count the minutes between the minute hand and the 12 o'clock position.

This activity will help children to:

- relate the position of the minute hand of a clock to a shape that is a fraction of a circle

- talk about times that are past and to the hour.

You will need these resources:

- copy the resource sheet on page 108 onto card (enlarged if you wish) and cut out the various pieces

- the large arrow takes the place of a minute hand

- a real, clear clock (with easily movable hands) may also be useful.

The activity

- Place the 'wheel of spokes' on the table, and upon it the large arrow at one of the times. It may be easiest to begin with the '5 past' idea.

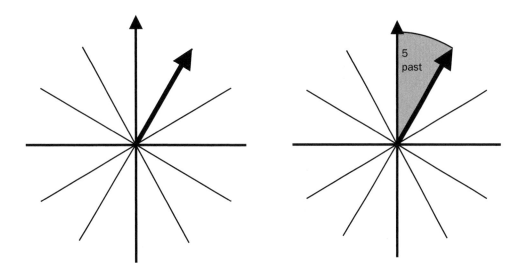

Which shape fits between the two arrows? 5 past.

- Repeat for each of the positions of the minute hand, asking the child to say out loud what the shape is that they are placing.

Extensions/alternatives

- The child chooses the position of the arrow instead of choosing the shape: *Where would you place the arrow if the time were 10 past? 25 to?*

- Use a real clock face instead of the 'wheel of spokes'.

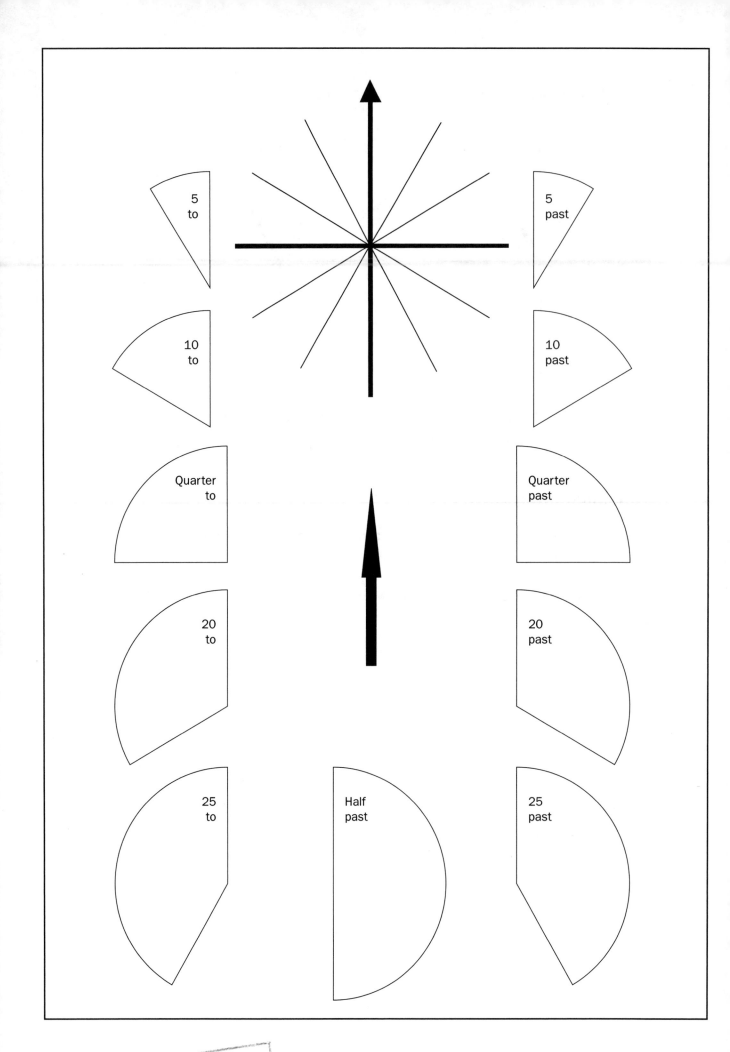

5 to

5 past

10 to

10 past

Quarter to

Quarter past

20 to

20 past

25 to

Half past

25 past

F. Understanding fractions

Fractions provide one of the biggest challenges for many children (and adults!) in understanding mathematics. Often the problem is a lack of understanding of the fraction notation (people commonly interchange ⅓ and ¾) or not recognising the relative values of fractions (some consider that because 4 is greater than 3, so ¼ is greater than ⅓). Calculating with fractions is also outside the intuitive thinking of many – multiplying fractions turns on its head the common view that multiplying makes numbers bigger, and the rules for adding fractions are regularly forgotten, so learners resort to adding both numerator and denominator, for example giving ½ + ⅓ = ⅖, which cannot be true as the result is less than the ½ we started with! Too often, learners have to work with the fraction notation in calculations long before they are ready to appreciate what is being represented.

The activities here offer different perspectives of fractions: as parts of a bar of chocolate, as parts of a circle, as parts of a number line and in comparing lengths. Through this imagery, learners should begin to have a better understanding of the meaning of fractions.

The number line activity has scope for moving onto adding fractions, with the fractions represented by physical objects, enabling learners to build a tangible picture of what happens when you add them.

The following activities are found in this section:

30. **Cuisenaire fractions: numbers up to ten** – using rod lengths to find fractions of numbers up to 10.

31. **Bars of chocolate** – find fractions of a shape – here it is a rectangle made up of a given number of squares (chunks of chocolate).

32. **Fractions of a number line** – building on the number line ideas, this time finding fractions of given lengths of lines.

33. **Images of fractions, using parts of a circle** – another way of recognising fractions, this time as parts of a circle, with the possibility of finding which fractions add up to make a whole one.

Cuisenaire fractions: numbers up to ten

This activity builds on the ideas used in activity 21, 'Factor walls', which helped children find factors of numbers. This time we find fractions of lengths using the same materials (Cuisenaire rods or the resource sheet in activity 8 'Ten is greater than one'), and the same structure of fitting together the lengths of the rods.

The activity should help children to:

- find fractions of the numbers up to 10

- handle fractions such as halves, thirds and quarters but the activity will progress naturally to enable children to handle all fractions up to tenths

- match the written notation with the spoken fractions

- write their own fraction notation.

You will need these resources:

- Cuisenaire Rods or the printed lengths from 1 cm to 10 cm (see resource sheet on page 31) to be copied onto card, and cut out

- some written fractions on cards (a selection of these can be found on the resource sheet on page 114).

The activity

- Take the 6 cm rod and pick out a few of the 3 cm rods.

    How many of these 3 cm rods will fit into the 6 cm rod? **Two**.

- Place the rods together as below.

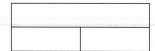

- Now place the cards '1' and '½' next to the rods, stating that if we call the larger rod a whole one, the smaller rods are both halves:

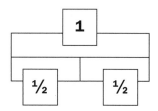

- *Why does the '½' have a '2' in the symbol?* **You need two halves to make a whole one/the one is shared into two parts/the whole one is divided by two.** The fraction symbol looks like a division sign.

Extension tasks

There are different ways in which this activity could develop.

- You could find the other rods that can be halved easily – the even lengths 2 cm, 4 cm, 8 cm and 10 cm – and reinforce the idea of a half. For example, with the 8 cm rod:

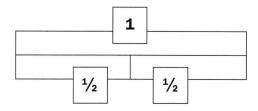

- You could explore other fractions of the 6 cm rod. For example, using the 6 cm and 2 cm rods:

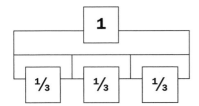

Why is there a '3' in the fraction? **There are three of the smaller rods that fit into the larger rod.**

- You could explore the fractions of each of the rods. There is a possibility of finding the fractions up to tenths. For example, using the longest and shortest rods:

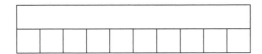

- If the child is ready to write their own notation, this could be the time to ask:

  How many little rods fit the larger one? **10.**

  What fraction is the smaller rod of the larger one? **One tenth.**

  How should we write the cards to show one tenth?

1/4	1/4	1/5
1/4	1/4	1/5
1/2	1/3	1/5
1/2	1/3	1/5
1	1/3	1/5

Bars of chocolate

This is a way of helping children to understand and use fractions.

The activity will help children to:

- see parts of a rectangle as fractions

- understand that fractions mean equal parts of a whole

- discuss the fraction notation

- find simple fractions of 12 (such as half, third or a quarter), and later, fractions of other numbers such as 10, 16 or 20.

You will need these resources:

- prepare some (interlocking) cubes, or use 5 cm card squares made up from activity 20, 'Make a rectangle'.

The activity

- Ask the children to build a bar of chocolate of 12 cubes (chunks).

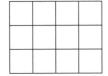

Can you break this bar into halves? **For example:**

Can you do it in a different way – making different shapes? **For example:**

How many different ways can you find half? **For example:**

- The shapes do not have to be congruent (identical in shape) but simply have the same number of squares.

  How many pieces are there in a half of 12? **Six.**

- Try the same with other fractions:

  Find different ways to break the bar into quarters. Break the bar into four equal pieces.

  Do all the pieces look the same?

  How many pieces are there in a quarter of the bar? **Three.**

  Why is a quarter of a bar written as ¼? **The notation means one shared into four parts; or 1 divided by 4; the fraction notation looks like the division sign [÷].**

  Find different ways to break the bar into thirds.

How many pieces are there in a third of the bar? **Four**.

Why is a third written as ⅓? **It means a whole one shared into three parts**.

Are there other fractions of the bar that you can make? **For example, sixths, twelfths**.

Extensions: finding fractions of other quantities

● Change the size of the bar of chocolate.

What fractions can you easily find, using 16 cubes? **You can make halves (eight pieces), quarters (four pieces), eighths (two pieces), and sixteenths (one piece)**.

Can you share this bar fairly between three people? **Not exactly – there is one piece left over**.

What fractions can you find using 10 cubes, 20 cubes etc?

Fractions of a number line

This is a way of helping children to understand fraction concepts, including fraction notation, equivalent fractions, and the relative sizes of fractions. This is a good activity for children to work in pairs or threes.

This activity will help children to:

- identify positions for simple fractions on a number line

- find fractions of quantities or numbers

- explain what is meant by a fraction of a line

- find equivalent fractions and explain their equivalence

- begin to order fractions, by saying which is greater or smaller

- measure lengths of lines.

You will need these resources:

- prepare a 24 cm line drawn on cm-squared paper (making sure that the line is drawn from dot to dot or from the junctions of the squares). Mark a 0 (zero) at the beginning and 1 (one) at the other end of the line (see the following diagram)

- make up some coloured card cut to lengths that relate to the fractions; for example, several strips cut at 6 cm in one colour (to represent ¼), several more in another colour to represent ⅓ (8 cm) and so on.

The activity

If the start of the line is 0, and the end of the line is 1, where would you place a half?

• The child may place a finger or pencil mark at the middle and need the answer confirmed; for example, by counting the same number of centimetre squares (12) from the middle to both the start and the end.

• To help, you could give the child two cards of 12 cm length that are marked '½', so that they could place both cards along the line, marking where they join, for example:

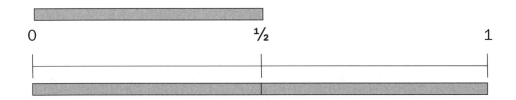

Where would you place a quarter of the line?

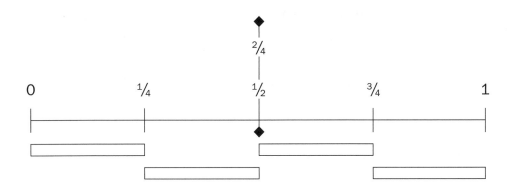

• Again, using the cards would help the child get a picture of the quarters, meaning that you need four of them to fit into a whole one.

• *How about three-quarters?* Using three '¼' card strips (6 cm long) would help the child to place the figure '¾' at the correct place on the line.

  What happens with two-quarters? **It is the same as ½.**

• Now try some other fractions, again using strips of card to help the child locate their positions.

Can you find where to place one-third? Two-thirds?

Look at the positions of a half, a third, a quarter and so on. Where might you place one-eighth on the line? Why should it come before one-sixth? Could you place one-hundredth on the line?

Where would you place seven-eighths?

What are all the fractions you can find, using whole centimetres?

- Soon, children will see that some fractions fall at the same positions.

  What fractions come at the same place as a half? **For example, ¾, ⅜, ⅛, ⁶⁄₁₂** (if they get that far).

  Do you notice anything the same about all these fractions? **The bottom number (denominator) is double the top number (numerator).**

  What fractions come at the same place as a quarter? **For example, two-eighths, three-twelfths.**

  What is the same about all these fractions? **Multiply the top number (numerator) by four, and you get the bottom number (denominator).**

- Further questions to promote mathematical reasoning:

  What length is ¼ of 24 cm? What amount is ¼ of £24?

  What other fractions of 24 can you find?

  Is ⅝ greater or less than ½?

  What fraction is 12 of 24? What fraction is 10 of 24?

  Why is it hard to find one-fifth of this line?

Extension

- Try lengths of lines other than 24 cm. The different lengths of lines will enable the child to explore different simple fractions. For example, a 20 cm line will give halves, quarters, fifths and tenths (if using whole centimetres), because 2, 4, 5 and 10 are factors of 20, whereas a 15 cm line will give thirds and fifths because 3 and 5 are factors of 15.

Adding fractions

● Using the cards, identify what fractions of the line they are.

Which card is ⅓ of the line? Which is ½?

● Put the cards together, next to the line, so that you are adding ½ and ⅓. Where do they reach? What does ½ + ⅓ = ?

Can you use the cards to help add other fractions?

Images of fractions, using parts of a circle

Children should have opportunities to see fractions in many ways, and this activity adds another perspective, to go along with number lines, parts of rods/lengths and rectangular blocks.

This activity will help children to:

● find fractions of a circle

● understand fraction notation

● compare sizes of fractions

● begin to add fractions.

You will need these resources:

● the resource sheet on page 124 shows a range of parts of circles: halves, thirds, quarters, sixths, eighths and twelfths. Copy the sheet onto card, and cut out the pieces ready for use

● blank circles of the same diameter.

The activity

● Spread out the pieces into sets – sets of halves, thirds, quarters and so on. The various fractions on the sheet are shaded differently to help children see the differences. Ask the child to use the card pieces to make whole circles. *Find as many different arrangements that you can.*

- Of course, children may start by using similar parts – for example, all thirds, or all quarters – to make a circle. However, there are some mixed combinations that will work. Children can fit the parts onto the blank circles given.

Questions

How many thirds do you need to make a whole circle?

How many quarters/sixths/eighths/twelfths?

Can you mix the parts? Which ones work?

How many quarters make a half?

How many sixths make a third?

Are there any other fractions you can link this way?

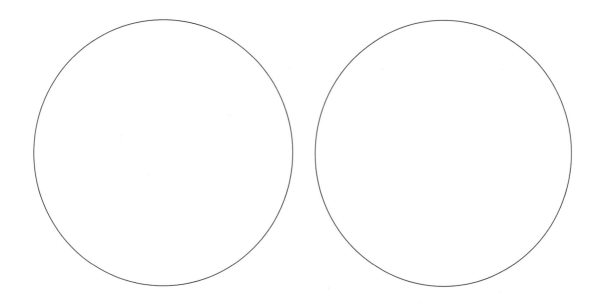